Human Rights and the Climate Crisis

An approach to guide our survival

Julián Correcha Rodríguez

for Sophie Helena,
my inspiration and dearest teacher

CONTENTS

ACKNOWLEDGMENTS

My gratitude is with my *Alma mater*, the Universidad Externado de Colombia, which provided some of my human rights foundations. My other academic experiences include the Universidad de los Andes, Bogotá, the Latrobe University Language Centre in Melbourne, and the University of Melbourne.

Aside from my studies, this book was inspired by the people I met growing up in Colombia, the resilient people from all over the world I have met and worked with in Australia, and the diverse people I have met in my travels.

Professors and academics have also been a source of inspiration. My appreciation and gratitude go to Christine Chinkin, Dianne Otto, Hilary Charlesworth, Lavanya Rajamani, Michelle Foster, Kirsty Gover, Erica Grundell, the Honourable Justice Michael Kirby, César Rodríguez-Garavito, Jairo Rivera-Sierra, Ernesto Rengifo García, William Namen, Felipe De Vivero Arciniegas, Vladimiro Naranjo Mesa, and Fernando Hinestrosa Daza.

I am deeply grateful to my parents Franklin and Helena, two beautiful teachers who, despite the history of conflict in Colombia and its consequent difficulties, managed to protect and raise three socially and environmentally conscious boys.

To my brothers Manuel and Leonardo, I could not be prouder of you. Despite distance and personal circumstances, the brotherhood, love, and friendship have always been there.

My heartfelt thanks to Claudia, Carlos and the Argentinian-Italian-Australian family in Melbourne who have embraced me since Manuel and my sister-in-law Valerie introduced us 20 years ago.

Thanks also to my mum-in-law Ros (or *Rosita*), who has been a close friend and always supportive of my Aussie journey.

And to the memory of Daryl. He was my father-in-law, a family man, and a bloody good mate.

I am most grateful to my wife Louise, editor of this book, and a continuous inspiration not only to keep improving my English writing and editing skills, but to be a better husband and father to our daughter Sophie Helena – a wonderful child that keeps me thinking about the kind of world she, and the ones not yet born, will hopefully live in.

INTRODUCTION

The effects of climate change are no longer something we might face in the future. We're facing them now. Increasing sea levels, severe cyclones and thunderstorms and more frequent fires, floods and droughts are affecting millions worldwide.

In Australia, we are still coming to terms with the consequences of the 2019–2020 bushfires. In the states of New South Wales, Queensland, the Australian Capital Territory and Victoria, for example, there have been an estimated 400 excess human deaths attributable to the aftermath of bushfire smoke[1].

These bushfires alone burnt over 24 million hectares. More than 3,000 homes were destroyed, and nearly three billion animals were killed or displaced. Many threatened species and other ecological communities were extensively harmed.[2] Putting the size of that devastation in perspective, the area of the UK is 24,249,500 hectares. Imagine. An area the size of England, Scotland, Wales, and Northern Ireland, destroyed by fires.

Of course, it's not just fires. Throughout February, May and July 2022, rainwater and flooding affected thousands in Queensland and New South Wales.

Clearly, Australia's disaster outlook is alarming. In 2020, climate and hazard risk analysts at the Cross Dependency Initiative found that 383,300 Australian properties could be classified as being at high risk of exposure to natural hazards. This number is projected to rise to 736,654 by 2100 – and that's not even including new developments.[3]

As is also happening worldwide, thousands will die due to climate change in the near future, while our political leaders continue to support the fossil fuel industry. How much more devastation do we need to see? We must lower our greenhouse gas emissions and phase out coal, oil and gas – not in 20 or 50 years, but now.

We also need to understand that climate change is not just an environmental issue; it's a human rights one too. Because it's not just

---

1 N B Arriagada, A J Palmer and others 'Unprecedent smoke-related health burden associated with the 2019-20 bushfires in eastern Australia' (The Medical Journal of Australia MJA Vol 213, Issue 6 pp 282– 283 https://onlinelibrary.wiley.com/doi/10.5694/mja2.50545

2 Royal Commission into National Natural Disaster Arrangements Report 28 Oct 2020, p5 https://naturaldisaster.royalcommission.gov.au/publications/royal-commission-national-natural-disaster-arrangements-report

3 Ibid, p70

about the number of people who have lost and will continue to lose their fundamental right to life because of climate change. It's also about respecting people's dignity, which is at the core of the human rights movement.

Climate change issues such as water scarcity, ocean acidification, loss of biodiversity and rising sea levels are not just ecological issues. They result in significant socio-political issues, including more internally displaced people (IDPs), conflict, and potential social collapse.

Millions are currently displaced, and the numbers continue to increase. People are losing their land as well as their cultures, livelihoods, rights to a dignified life, and humanity. And as we watch and let that happen, we are losing ours too.

The devastating effects of climate change are compromising our fundamental human rights, so it's essential we look at climate change with a human rights lens too. We also need to make sure there is a high level of compliance with these rights, as well as mechanisms to ensure that when there are violations, people are truly held accountable.

And so, this book is my attempt to analyse the cultural, social and economic problems we are facing as a global collective, from a human rights perspective. I believe it's time to take stock and look at what is no longer working in our societies if we are to have any hope of addressing our global challenges and tackling climate change. After all, we caused this, and we need to take collective action to fix it. So why haven't we? One reason could be that we've been focusing on treating the symptoms rather than the human causes of climate change. And that we need to change that focus back to the core of what makes us human, what guides our behaviours, and what makes our societies function the way they do. Because in the end, we can't fix anything if we don't first find what's broken.

Climate change requires us to move away from all our binary lenses, including being on the right or left side of politics. We need to collectively address the global challenges we have created.

We need to truly work together.

As a father thinking of future generations, I felt it was my duty to make my small contribution to the discussion on this issue. Because I know that soon, my daughter will look into my eyes and ask me what I did about climate change. And I want to have an answer for her.

I hope this book inspires others – including our leaders – to consider how they too might answer such a question.

After all, it's not just human rights at stake – it's our survival.

.

1
AN OVERVIEW OF HUMAN RIGHTS

Human rights appear in the legal history of humankind only after the second world war. Indeed, the creation of the United Nations (UN) and its charter and preamble on the 24th of October 1945[4] constitute an acknowledgement of the principle of human rights universality[5] as well as certain fundamental aspects of human rights, such as the dignity of all human beings and the equality of men and women.

The subsequent Universal Declaration of Human Rights (UDHR), proclaimed by the General Assembly of the UN in 1948, also reiterates the universality of human rights, their natural law foundation and their historical importance to achieving peace and security.

However, after World War Two, the world was still in the process of decolonisation, and it is arguable that in many of these colonies, human rights were not recognised or respected – in fact, it seems the notion of human rights universality and its application were simply not there. Many of what were then colonies in Asia and Africa, for example, did not participate in the debates and proclamation of international human rights, and as such, may have perceived human rights as an imposition and not as universal principles.[6]

---

4 United Nations, Charter of the United Nations (October 1945) http://www.un.org/en/sections/un-charter/preamble/index.html
5 According to the Oxford Dictionary, universality is "the quality of involving or being shared by all people or things in the world or in a particular group; the quality of being true in or appropriate for all situations."
6 P Alston and R Goodman 'International Human Rights' (Oxford University Press 4th ed 2013) pp 146–147

Even today, the application of human rights universality could be up for questioning. After all, the treatment of some minorities worldwide – Indigenous groups and refugees, for example – continues to be appalling. For instance, the exodus from Myanmar to Bangladesh of thousands of Rohingya due to the systematic attacks of Myanmarese security forces, and the lack of political will from their government to stop this ethnic cleansing, seem to add to this point. A more recent example is the unjustified invasion of Ukraine by Russia.

Human rights and the schools of thought

To better understand the notion of the universality of human rights, it is relevant to mention what professor of law and anthropology Marie-Bénédicte Dembour says on the four schools of human rights thought – namely, that "natural scholars conceive of human rights as given; deliberative scholars as agreed upon; protest scholars as fought for; and discourse scholars as talked about."[7]

According to Ms Dembour, the natural scholars consider the universality of human rights as something that comes from nature. Most natural scholars have moral and religious fundaments based on the premise of God or a supreme source – they believe in the existence of human rights per se, and some accept the importance of their recognition through legislative instruments. Thus, for them, "legal consensus can only ever be the proof of the existence of human rights, not a foundation of human rights."

Deliberative scholars seem to be more pragmatic, she observes, following perhaps the ideas of philosophers like Jean-Jacques Rosseau and his social contract, where rights and obligations come to fruition when societies agree upon them.

For the protest scholars, as there are so many injustices worldwide and seemingly not enough answers and solutions to the problems affecting people's basic human rights, there will always be another fight to join in the name of justice.

It is said also that the discourse scholars do not believe in human rights to begin with, but instead "repeatedly point to the shortcomings of the human rights discourse that does not deliver what it promises, namely, equality between human beings."

---

7 Marie-Benedicte Dembour 'What are Human Rights? Four Schools of Thought (2010) 32 Human Rights Quarterly 1, pp 1,3,6,8

All four of the schools of thought appear to have some logical reasoning and validity. I believe there is no way to categorically say that one school "holds the truth" or is better than the others – they're all important to understand and consider.

Does human rights universality apply to East and West?

A conceptual universality of human rights is shared by natural scholars and people who have religious or spiritual beliefs – and there doesn't seem to be much separation between eastern and western countries in this respect. As Harvard Professor of Law Mary Ann Glendon suggests, according to the findings of a group of UNESCO philosophers who had consulted with Confucian, Hindu, Muslim and European thinkers, "a core of fundamental principles was widely shared in countries that had not yet adopted rights instruments and in cultures that had not embraced the language of rights."[8]

In addition, to say that human rights only respond to the interest and values of the west seems to ignore history.

The aforementioned Universal Declaration of Human Rights (or UDHR) acknowledges both the individual approach of the west, with civil and political rights as expressed in the International Covenant on Civil and Political Rights (ICCPR), and the collective, community-orientated approach of the east, with economic, social and cultural rights expressed in the International Covenant on Economic and Social and Cultural Rights (ICESCR).[9]

The interconnectedness of both international covenants is also widely recognised. Thus, the premise of human rights universality seems not only to reside in the diverse religious worldwide but in the core of human rights principles that have been influenced by both eastern and western approaches. However, human rights universality is clearer when international treaties that recognise them are ratified by the state members and incorporated into their respective domestic legislations.

This consensual sense of universality may have more weight given that all 193 UN member States have ratified at least one of the core human rights treaties, and 80% have ratified four or more. As the UN Office of the High Commissioner writes, this reflects the consent of States, creates legal obligations for them and gives "concrete

---

8 Alston and Goodman op.cit. p 146.
9 Ibid p 277.

expression to universality."[10]

Clearly, the roots of the universality of human rights are found in cultural, historical and legal characteristics that apply to both the east and the west.

As Alston and Goodman reflect in their definitive International Human Rights, "what made universal human rights possible – was the similarity among all human beings. Their starting point was the simple fact of the common humanity shared by every man, woman and child on earth, a fact that, for them, put linguistic, racial, religious, and other differences into their proper perspective"[11]. Given this, it appears that progress towards a better common understanding of human rights, and the implementation of human rights universality, will continue in both the east and the west.

However, with widespread globalisation and the free-market economic approach, this progressive implementation of universal human rights will be a complex challenge to tackle in the decades to come.[12]

From a practical point of view, the notion of universality could apply when citizens and governments worldwide understand the historical importance of human rights, and when the principles and human rights conventions are upheld and integrated as part of the culture of the respective states; when they develop an understanding that human rights are not static but rather living instruments, subject to changing interpretations depending on how societies and human beings evolve.[13]

Considering that many human rights violations still occur in developing and developed countries in both the east and the west, there is still a need from both eastern and western developed countries to show more leadership in the ratification and implementation of fundamental human rights. Having an understanding that fundamental human rights have a progressive implementation, as well as ensuring western approaches respect and appreciate the differences of the eastern countries, is also fundamental to achieving stability and peace.

The application of the universality of human rights, however, may

---

10 United Nations Office of the High Commissioner, What are human rights? Universal and inalienable
http://www.ohchr.org/EN/Issues/Pages/WhatareHumanRights.aspx
11 Alston and Goodman op. cit. p 149.
12 Ibid p 278
13 Ibid p 544

only occur when we as collective interconnected societies learn more about the history of our planet and different societies. When we learn to appreciate the beauty and uniqueness of every culture, and honour and respect the inherent dignity of every human being on this planet. When bullying and discrimination perhaps cease to exist and are no longer even in our vocabulary. Only then – when and if we decide to walk that path – may we move from formal, legalistic equality to a more egalitarian global village where substantial equality is applied.

Currently though, our global economy and socio-economic structures seem to be characterised by the relevance we give to competitiveness. It doesn't matter whether we're in Australia, China, India, Japan, Africa, Europe, or South, Central or North America, we all tend to believe that we are right, and "they" are wrong. This sense of competitiveness and pseudo-nationalistic belief that "we" are superior or that we hold the truth, which unfortunately education and even religions feed on, has led humankind to some of the most horrendous atrocities.

Cultural, social and economic rights

Historically, when government leaders talk about human rights, they tend to talk about individual rights, or those reflected in ICCPR. This covenant was adopted after the second world war and is the one most people think of when they think of human rights, perhaps because it is the one most governments give most importance to (at least throughout the western world). These rights include the right to life, the right to freedom of thought, conscience and religion, and the understanding that all persons are equal before the law without any discrimination to the equal protection of the law. They outline, among others, our rights to not be subjected to torture or slavery or cruel, inhuman or degrading treatment or punishment.

These rights are of course fundamental, and we should continue to uphold them. However, we see again and again that this does not always happen. Why? Putting aside for a moment deeper philosophical reflections on our true human nature, I think there's something else we're missing in focusing on striving for individual rights only. Perhaps of power, and of privilege, and of all the factors that need to be in place for individual rights to be respected – yet which continue to elude us.

Let me explain. You may have been through, or know someone who has experienced, a situation where they knew their rights were being compromised, but what they stood to lose by standing up for those rights was greater. Whether it's an international student afraid to lose their dream for a different future by speaking up against an underpaying employer, or any of the tragic or dangerous decisions people around the world have to make every day just to survive under economic and social conditions that give them no viable alternative, it's clear we need to face why so many are left in a position of not being able to stand up for their individual rights in the first place, and why others know they can take advantage of that.

In other words, I believe we don't properly acknowledge the social, cultural and economic factors that need to actually be in place before all humans will be able to enjoy individual human rights.

Because even if it does seem simplistic – and in this, I don't wish to minimise anyone's challenges – it's a lot easier to make the individual decision to reduce your carbon footprint by applying for a loan to buy an electric car to drive to work as a woman in a country where you enjoy the freedom to do all of those things, than as a woman in a place where you can't do any of them without risking your life. It's easier to stand up for your rights as an employee in a country that would support you financially if you lost that job. To care about recyclable packaging when you're not holding the only food you might have that day.

The narrow approach of identifying human rights only with individual rights has also led to an increasingly selfish, individualistic mentality and approaches that are reflected in:

- A global economic system that continues to widen the gap between rich and poor, and in which the very elements of a social contract of democracy are being eroded.
- Many governments worldwide representing the short-term interests of corporations. Subsidies and tax exemptions abound for these entities, and every time there is a financial crisis, it is the people that end up having to bail them out.
- The increasing disintegration of the social fabric that makes people believe and respect the law, institutions and their leaders. In other words, the erosion of public faith in democracy. To even have a chance of reversing this, government accountability, transparency and upholding ethical values are more critical than ever.[14]

---

14 Freedom House, Government Accountability & Transparency 'A well-functioning democracy requires strong safeguards against official corruption' https://freedomhouse.org/issues/government-accountability-transparency

ICESCR and ICCPR – why balance is crucial

So where do we start? I think we need to start with an understanding of how we have so far come short in the application, implementation and progressive compliance of one of the main international human rights instruments that focuses on the creation of these broader economic and social conditions – ICESCR.

After the catastrophic effects of the first and second world war, the United Nations and the leaders of the world understood that to avoid further conflict and more wars, it was imperative for nations worldwide to adopt not only ICCPR but the equally important ICESCR, because it is within ICESCR that many of the foundations of development and social policy are laid.

Some of the most fundamental acknowledgements laid out in ICESCR include the equal right of men and women to the enjoyment of all economic, social and cultural rights recognised in the covenant, including the right to work; of a decent living with fair wages and just, safe and healthy working conditions; the right to social security; the widest possible protection and assistance to the family as a fundamental unit of society, with special protection to mothers during before and after childbirth; the enjoyment of the highest attainable standard of physical and mental health; and the right of everyone to an education.

If governments complied with ICESCR properly, the taxes we all pay or should pay – whether as individuals or business entities – should cover the public housing, roads, schools, hospitals, education, childcare and aged care many of us so desperately need.

But we seem to have left ICESCR behind in our striving for the individual rights in ICCPR. One reason for this could be ICESCR's association with collectivist societies, and a potential fear that has therefore developed around words like 'collectivist'. ICESCR, however, has been adopted by most nations worldwide and remains the instrument that most effectively fosters the circumstances that need to exist for people to be able to enjoy the individual rights in ICCPR. It's the missing piece of the puzzle; the foundation upon which ICCPR can truly exist and work.

But maybe there's something else that we need to tackle. Something that's perhaps even more confronting to face.

As mentioned, compliance with ICESCR should mean that there are more than enough resources for a society to be at the level of development in which the collective, and the individuals within it, can thrive. Or at the very least, not just strive to survive. However, due to the tax evasion, subsidies, and corruption symptomatic of a tip too far on the scales towards the interests of the individual – and in particular, a select few – this is not the case.

Instead, we are increasingly seeing the brunt of adequate basic public services being borne by some of our poorest, while others more fortunate continue to profess their support for the rights of the individual – comfortable, perhaps, in their knowledge of what truly needs to happen to make those rights a reality for most.

Leaving behind our binary lenses, this is not about making a case or advocating for the "supremacy" of ICESCR over the ICCPR; to be able to enjoy fundamental human rights, both ICCPR and ICESCR need to be included and respected. This interconnectedness of both ICCPR and ICESCR is in fact widely accepted as necessary to protect fundamental human rights.[15]

Looking more closely now at how a greater respect for some of the fundamental rights expressed in ICESCR could contribute to alleviating the climate crisis, consider that substantial gender equality is important for many reasons, but particularly for increasing the number of people with higher levels of education. This, it has been shown, generally leads to fewer socio-economic struggles and less conflict. It also creates the conditions in which individual decisions for the good of the environment, others and the future – rather than one's immediate survival – can more comfortably be made.

Finally, it leads to something we do need to discuss more openly, which is people being less inclined to have more children, thus reducing the population to be sustained by our planet. Of course, such discussions need to be led with love and an understanding of the complex social factors that underpin decisions around procreation, but they still need to be had. In the end, it is through genuine and substantial gender equality that we create more equal societies with lower populations and less $CO2$ production, which will substantially reduce the effects of climate change.

We haven't yet been successful in the adoption nor the application, implementation of and progressive compliance with ICESCR by some

15 Alston and Goodman op. cit. p 277.

key states, because we've been focused on individual rights while disregarding the need for more inclusive, collective understandings and approaches.

To tackle the global challenges we have created, a holistic approach is essential – one that integrates a shift in our common understandings. We need a more collective rather than individualistic and anthropocentric worldview, and to embrace inclusiveness in all areas of life – economically, culturally, socially and politically.

Equally, respecting Indigenous rights is fundamental to better coping with climate change. Indeed, both historically and now, and not just in Australia or the Americas but worldwide, Indigenous communities and leaders have been killed, displaced and systematically disempowered. Their lands have been exploited by multinationals for natural resources including oil, gas and coal (and yes, precisely the ones that we need to stop digging).

This also must change, and soon.

2
HUMANITY AND GLOBAL CHALLENGES

Addressing our global challenges requires us to be better informed and have a more objective understanding of our past, as well as come to terms with our current reality. This will be crucial to helping us move forward into a sustainable future, the only one we might have.

Throughout the 1960s and 70s, scientists and the fossil fuel industry knew about climate change. But unlike the scientific community, who has spent the intervening decades telling us about its devastating effects, the fossil fuel industry's approach to climate change has generally been to criticise the "uncertainty of science" and basically deny its existence.

And until recently, with the complicity of the media and the fossil fuel industry, many governments worldwide were doing the same. But now that there's no longer any way to keep denying the effects of climate change, their approach and strategy have shifted, with their main argument now focusing on the need to protect their economies. Apparently, that is done by protecting those jobs the fossil fuel industry provides…

The reaction of many nations thus far to climate change has generally been to either believe that scientific advancements would save us from extinction at some indeterminate point in the future, or that we are doomed. In both scenarios, climate change seems to be considered so big that there's nothing we can do for now, so we may as well continue with business as usual.

There are also many of us who think that the devastating effects of climate change are likely to be experienced at a point far away in space and time, perhaps in 50–100 or more years, so what is there to be concerned about now, if we are not going to live through it?

Of course, this is not true. Climate change has already affected millions of people worldwide. It has caused and is causing financial, physical and psychological damage. These irresponsible common attitudes also seemingly shared by government and business leaders are not only unethical and inhumane, they may also be illegal.

Indeed, many people, including Australian medical doctors, rightly consider climate change a public health emergency.[16] And businesses, due to the pressure of investors, regulators, and activist groups, are starting to understand the importance of considering and disclosing the risks that climate change will have on their economic activities and how management will respond to it. This is in line with considerations of directors' potential liability for breaching their legal duties of care and due diligence when climate change risk is not properly managed.[17]

We must start acting now and, without any remorse, effectively leave behind the fossil fuel economy and fully embrace an economy that substantially integrates renewable means of energy. It's not only the most logical but quite likely the only way to effectively reduce our greenhouse gas emissions and reduce the impact of climate change, giving us some window of opportunity to survive on planet Earth.

So, what actually is climate change? The following analogy, which you may already have heard, could be helpful in answering that.

Imagine a gas stove heating a saucepan of water. If you keep the gas on, eventually the water will start spilling out, as well as evaporating until it reaches a point where the gas must be turned off. But on Earth, not only have we not turned off the gas, we haven't even turned it down. On the contrary, we keep turning it up.

In 1992 the Rio Framework Convention on Climate Change called

---

16 Doctors for the Environment Australia, letter dated 11 August 2020 addressed to the Hon. Scott Morrison, MP, Prime Minister of Australia https://www.dea.org.au/wp-content/uploads/2020/08/2020-08-06-Healthy-Recovery-Letter-_-Scott-Morrison-PM.pdf
17 Deloitte 'Clarity in Financial Reporting – Disclosure of climate-related risks' (A&A Accounting Technical Feb 2020) https://www2.deloitte.com/content/dam/Deloitte/au/Documents/audit/deloitte-au-audit-clarity-disclosure-climate-related-risks-070220.pdf and Australian Broadcasting Corporation ABC 'Rest Super Fund Commits to net-zero emission investments after Brisbane man sues' 2 Nov 2020 https://www.abc.net.au/news/2020-11-02/rest-super-commits-to-net-zero-emmissions/12840204

for developed countries to pay the cost of limiting greenhouse gas emissions in developing countries. We did not do that, and we continued finding excuses to not switch to renewable means of energy.

One of the climate change scientists who has been proving the devastating effects of climate change and advocating for a better understanding of it – and for real action – is Dr James E Hansen. He is a former director of the NASA Goddard Institute for Space Studies, and currently Director of the Climate Science Awareness and Solutions program of the Columbia University Earth Institute. One of Dr Hansen's key recommendations, along with several other high-profile scientists, has been the need to capture CO_2 emissions and keep them below 350 ppm[18] to avoid catastrophic climate change effects. However, we had already exceeded the 350ppm by 1987[19]. So, it's now been more than 30 years of exceeding the 350ppm limit.

We haven't decreased emissions. Indeed, according to the National Aeronautics and Space Administration (NASA), these are some of the carbon emissions recorded since 2005[20]:

October 2005: 380 ppm
October 2010: 390 ppm
October 2015: 401 ppm
October 2018: 409 ppm
October 2019: 411 ppm
October 2020: 415 ppm
May 2022: 418 ppm
July 2022: 419 ppm

Most of the scientific community is certain that the main force of climate change is carbon emissions. Emissions that stay in the atmosphere for thousands of years, hence the imperative need to limit them and efficiently phase down fossil fuel emissions and transition to carbon-free energies now.

However, some of the wealthiest among us appear to believe they might escape the effects of climate change from the comfort of their mansions. But effects such as rising sea levels rise will not only continue to affect the Pacific and Torres Strait islands, they'll affect

---

18 Ibid
19 C Sagan, 'Billions and Billions – Thoughts on Life and Death at the Brink of the Millennium' (Random House New York 1st Edition 1997) p 106.
20 The National Aeronautics and Space Administration- NASA 'Facts - Vital Signs' https://climate.nasa.gov/vital-signs/carbon-dioxide/

every coastline city in the world.

The potential ecological and societal collapse needs to be considered deeply.[21] So far, the answers have been to invest more heavily in police, army (law and order), and the mistaken belief that supporting the fossil fuel industries and more autocratic types of government is the way to move forward. Clearly, it's not.

The rising prominence of climate crisis and ecological degradation is also seen in the number of litigation cases related to climate change. In the U.S. alone, there are currently 1,559 climate change litigation cases: 863 federal statutory claims, 79 constitutional claims, 384 state law claims, 27 common law claims, 27 public trust claims, 35 securities and financial regulations, 1 trade agreement, 97 adaptation claims, and 46 cases by climate change protesters and scientists[22].

There is now more than ever the need to develop better and more informed understandings of the socio-ecological interconnections on planet Earth. As the economist and professor Kate Raworth puts it, "rather than wait for growth to clean it up – because it won't – it is far smarter to create economies that are regenerative by design, restoring and renewing the local-to-global cycles of life on which human well-being depends."[23]

Climate change is also making people scared, withdrawn, and living in denial. In Australia particularly, many in both politics and the community seem to prefer the "no worries, mate, she'll be right" attitude – without consciously understanding what we are doing or perhaps not doing.

We live in a global economy and our current challenges are global, but our societies and nations are not acting globally.

One of the main opportunities we have to tackle climate change is cultural – and relates to questioning our beliefs. I believe we could awaken our curiosity as a species and learn to not just tolerate but really appreciate the diversity of the cultures, ethnicities and historical legacies of the different regions or nations of the world. It is only this way, I believe, that we might be able to avoid making the same mistakes

---

21 J Bendell 'Deep Adaptation: A Map for Navigating Climate Tragedy' (Institute of Leadership and Sustainability (IFLAS) University of Cumbria UK (2nd Edition released 27 July 2020) http://lifeworth.com/deepadaptation.pdf
22 Ibid
23 K Raworth 'Seven ways to Think Like a 21st Century Economist' (Chelsea Green Publishing 2017) pp 42,43,44,176; C Folke, et al 'Reconnecting to the Biosphere,' AMBIO 40 (2011) p 719.

our common ancestors made – including about our environment.

We must change our tendency to discriminate, create stereotypes, label, and put people in certain moulds so that they make sense according to our cultural, religious and world views. We need to move away from our monocultural views of planet Earth, characterised by our pride in the city, region, state or nation we were born into, as well as prejudice against those who look, sound or appear different from "us." From this place, we could create a cultural environment of respect and pride, not as inhabitants of certain nations, but as part of the human species.

Discrimination and structural social and economic inequalities (due in part to a lack of progressive compliance of ICESCR) are clearly seen in the number of deaths from COVID-19 not only in the developing world but also many parts of the developed world, evidencing our capitalism embracing the widening gap between rich and poor.

But let's not forget, we are in a race against the clock. The climate crisis cannot longer be ignored. Remember the school strikes that happened in many cities worldwide in 2019, supported by the C40 Cities Climate Leadership Group? When our children were teaching us all a lesson, demanding "system change, no climate change"? One of the billboards that stayed in my mind said: "You'll die of old age; I'll die of climate change." But the way things are looking now, I wouldn't even bet on us dying of old age.

It's possible to write a different story. To approach our challenges not only holistically but with a sense of humility and respect to fellow human beings and the diverse species inhabiting our planet.

We would need to start collectively asking what's in it for all of us? And what's in it for all of us not just now, but also for our children and their children?

I hope not only people in positions of power, but all of us as a collective, keep asking ourselves: What legacy do we want to leave?

To reduce the impacts of climate change, it is vital to understand that climate change has deepened other global challenges, and it also coexists with them. Climate change does not exist in isolation and is not only a problem for the scientific and research community or one that belongs only in the international law and diplomacy realms.

A holistic approach is required to tackle the global challenges, to have a chance of reducing the impact of climate change, and to have better odds for the survival of our species.

In the next chapters, I have grouped some of our most pressing global challenges into categories – cultural, social and economic. There is no order or hierarchy, as they are all interconnected. And as mentioned earlier, identifying, understanding, and acknowledging these global problems is essential to being able to tackle them – which is necessary if we are to decrease the impacts of climate change.

Our global challenges, including the climate crisis, will not disappear because we live in our own bubbles and don't see them, or because we consciously or subconsciously don't want to see them.

The words of Saudi Arabian astronaut Prince Sultan bin Salmon Al-Saud are worth repeating: "The first day or so, we all pointed to our countries. The third or fourth day, we were pointing to our continents. By the fifth day, we were aware of only one Earth."[24]

---

24 C Sagan, op. cit. p 136.

3

CULTURAL CHALLENGES AND OPPORTUNITIES

During my postgraduate studies and particularly after completing the subject climate change and human rights, I was overwhelmed by the conclusions of the scientific community. I was overwhelmed not only because of the scientific consensus of the severity of climate change and its effects, but because it clearly links to the existential threat the climate crisis brings to our species.

Questioning our beliefs

It is respectable to have our own opinions regarding the climate crisis, but this is science talking loud and clear. This is not about "my" or "your" opinion, neither "Do you think?" nor "Do you believe?" It is about facts and informing ourselves better.

However, after many conversations with friends and family members, perhaps like many who have been involved in or have studied climate change have also experienced, I felt I failed miserably to communicate the urgency and the changes that as a global community we require.

I painfully realised it is not about science, and how informed people are or want to be.

The real problem with climate change is cultural.

It is about our world views and the socio-economic understandings so ingrained in our minds. Our perception of reality and our shaped wants and needs. For instance, one of the most pressing systems to change is that of the patriarchy.

We all live in a patriarchal world. Patriarchy is widely supported by religions and our political and economic system. Achieving gender equality is vital in our race against the clock to try to reduce the effects of climate change in terms of saving human lives and increasing our chances of avoiding socio-economic and ecological collapse – women and children particularly in low-income countries are indeed more susceptible to suffer more deeply the effects of climate change. They are already millions who are currently homeless and internally displaced.

Historians and history keep telling us that when many people found themselves in unjust, extreme poverty conditions, and in state of despair, these are breeding grounds for revolts, revolutions and for heads being cut off.

The United States of America, for example, has ratified neither the International Covenant on Economic, Social and Cultural Rights (ICESCR) nor the Convention on the Elimination of All Forms of Discrimination Against Women (CEDAW). The Holy See (the Vatican) has also taken no action, ignoring these fundamental Treaties (as the UN ratification status dashboard[25] shows). Feel free to check on this dashboard what human rights conventions have already been adopted by the country you currently live in – keeping in mind that there are no legal obligations imposed on a signatory state. Indeed, signing the international agreement is the first step for states, the obligations to comply with a convention only start when the convention is ratified.

The real, differential, oppressive and discriminatory salary gap between males and females in most countries worldwide is also evidence of the patriarchy. The salary gap is also a clear violation of both international human rights conventions ICESCR and CEDAW.[26]

Women in most societies are not only expected but need to run most of their households, while holding down paid employment, because the household's financial income is simply not enough. This brings up the need to include, as part of whatever socio-economic system we come up with, the substantial and real compensation for the

---

25 United Nations Human Rights Office of The High Commissioner, Status of ratification interactive dashboard https://indicators.ohchr.org

26 International Covenant on Economic, Social and Cultural Rights, opened for signature 16 December 1966, 993 UNTS 3, Arts 2 (2), 3, 7 (a) (i)
https://www.ohchr.org/en/professionalinterest/pages/cescr.aspx; International Convention on the Elimination of All Forms of Discrimination Against Women, opened for signature 1 March 1980; United Nations, Article 11 (d)

work of running a home. After all, how would the "breadwinners" (although they are already disappearing) do their jobs if no one were doing the unpaid household work?

This is a historical debt we cannot continue to dismiss.

Our past shapes who we are and shapes our identity. We require not only a holistic approach and a shift in consciousness, but a redefinition of our identity too.

We need a more objective knowledge of our past, to develop a genuine appreciation and respect for those who have been historically discriminated against, including our Indigenous brothers and sisters, and to better understand our mistakes so that we can acknowledge and correct them.

The legacy of our patriarchal societies is part of our common history through the different empires, conquests and colonisation processes, and of course also WWI and WWII.

The need to dominate, to exert power, is something we must confront.

We may perhaps need to remind ourselves that the worst genocides and massacres in the history of humankind did not start with the killing acts themselves, but rather with bullying people and discriminating against minorities under the guise of the bullies' right to 'speak up for what was "right"'.

Imagine a world where countries are not invaded because a certain country supposedly has weapons of mass destruction, is an evil socialist country, is bringing "freedom" or is imposing economic sanctions that make countries so weak that a military coupe "is needed" to bring back "stability".

Authoritarian regimes (dictatorships) are well-known in the region I am originally from. Countries such as Argentina, Venezuela, Brazil, Chile, Colombia and Panama have had their share of them. In many cases, with the support or the laisse faire approach of the international community.

Historically, in such regimes, the winners are the corporations, shareholders and families in or close to power, while most people struggle daily for survival. Not to mention the violation of fundamental human rights – torture, killings and the creation of more refugees and internally displaced people (IDPs).

This is not something from our past world history or South America's history. It is happening as I am writing this book. 4.4 million

Venezuelans had to leave their country and went to neighbouring countries. Colombia alone is hosting 1.8 million of our Venezuelan sisters and brothers.[27]

I think collectively, we are coming to understand that conflict means business in itself. The military, security, weapons, and fossil fuel industries are at the core of our global economic system.

Historically, for most of the countries that were "set free" (or "invaded" depending on how you want to see it), this happened because of the wealth of their natural resources or their geopolitical situation.

It's sad but true – it's about domination, power and accessing natural resources. Just like the illegal invasion by Russia of Ukraine.

There is a conscious or subconscious belief that some people of our species are superior. Our extreme differences of social classes, and caste systems, and the fact that in both the "developed" and "developing world" we still have monarchies that exemplify this.

Selfishness, greed and a superiority complex are descriptive of our socio-political and economic system. One that if we do not change, will mean our children and grandchildren will have to carry the burden of a future non-liveable planet.

Substantial gender equality

For the United Nations Security Council to comply with its primary responsibility of the maintenance of international peace and security, it requires going to the origins of their Resolution 1325 on women and peace and security[28], and starting a real commitment to conflict prevention and a process of demilitarisation.

The need to properly address the cause of conflict is essential. Within that, achieving gender equality is paramount. But gender equality within a balanced understanding of intersectionality and inclusiveness. (Noting here that gender is only one aspect that shapes our identities; we also need to consider factors like nationality, ethnicity, Indigenous backgrounds, refugee and internally displaced people, political and religious affiliation, marital status, disability, age, and sexual orientation.)

---

27 Figures at a Glance, Office of the United Nations High Commissioner for Refugees
https://www.unhcr.org/figures-at-a-glance.html
28 United Nations Security Council Resolution 1325 (2000)
https://www.unwomen.org/en/docs/2000/10/un-security-council-resolution-1325

A basic reason for achieving gender equality is the fact that women who have access to education are more likely to have fewer children, delay having children and be better able to nourish and look after them when and if they do decide to have them – check out the Ted talk of Katharine Wilkinson for more on how empowering women and girls can help to reduce the effects of climate change.[29]

Gender equality = Educated women = Population control = Reduction of GHG emissions.

The above is exemplified in my own family tree and history. My grandmother (Mum's mum) had 14 children (9 women 5 men). Those were the times when women supposedly belonged in the kitchen, and as girls and young women, stayed at home helping their mums and looking after their siblings. Education and going to school were reserved for men, and women were generally expected to stay at home until they found someone to marry.

However, all my aunties managed to get an education. All of them had children too but on average two per family. Mum had three. My two brothers don't have children and they both so far have decided they do not want to bring children onto this planet. I have one child.

It is not only from a population control perspective, and the reduction of GHG emissions, but also substantial gender equality ensures peace processes last longer and that the likelihood for conflict to arise is reduced.[30]

Having been born and raised and seen different peace processes in Colombia, South America, it appears clear that proper access to education, employment, social security and adequate standards of living – in other words, compliance with ICESCR – means in regions of conflict or where conflict is likely to arise, people start to develop different understandings.

Indeed, people will start to see real solutions won't come about by using force, violence or physical means, but by being able to listen and look for conciliatory approaches and constructive scenarios. By destroying and demonising the "others", we only destroy ourselves and our sense of humanity. As it happens in our personal and family lives, so it happens in conflict and war. It is so easy to hurt and to damage, but so difficult to heal, rebuild and compensate.

---

29 K Wilkinson 'How empowering women and girls can help stop global warming.' TED Palm Spring California, November 2018, available at https://www.youtube.com/watch?v=vXJJEcrinwg
30 Preventing conflict transforming justice securing the peace – Global Study on the Implementation of United Nations Security Council Resolution 1325 (2015) (49)-(206)-(230).

Achieving gender equality is not a theoretical or philosophical but rather a practical matter, as it does substantially benefit countries. This is shown for instance in the current COVID-19 pandemic. Although it is still too soon to assess the damage, we can start to look at the results of the Nordic countries' responses. Iceland, Norway, Finland and Denmark, all led by female prime ministers, showed their leadership by the low number of deaths (low thousands combined by July 2021). On the other hand, Sweden, led by a male, had over ten thousand casualties by July 2021 (since November 2021, Sweden has had a female Prime Minister).

The importance of gender equality in all areas of life, but particularly in leadership positions, is not only clearly seen in the Nordic region, but also in many countries worldwide. Indeed, the high number of deaths caused by COVID-19 in the US, UK, Brazil, Russia, India, Iran, Italy, France, Turkey, Spain, Mexico, Peru, Argentina and Colombia, to name just a few, all under government of male leaders, evidenced the need for substantial gender equality.

The patriarchal, racist and structural socio-economic inequalities deeply rooted in our societies have played and continue to play a critical role in the numbers of COVID-19 casualties as well as the creation of more conflict and violence worldwide, as we continue to see on the news.

Discrimination

The discriminatory approach of our socio-economic system is seen in global levels of poverty, hunger, health, and the increasing number of IDPs and refugees worldwide

Poverty

The level of poverty our "civilisation" has allowed unfortunately shows the lack of progressive compliance with the International Covenant on Economic, Social and Cultural Rights. Figures from the World Bank speak loudly and clearly in this respect. According to the bank, in 2017, an estimated 9.2 per cent of the world's population lived on less than $1.90 a day.[31]

Perhaps we could ask ourselves, if we earned $2 or $4 per day, would that mean we are no longer poor?

It may be fair to say most of us do not want to discuss how many

---

31 World Bank, Measuring Poverty: https://www.worldbank.org/en/topic/measuringpoverty

dollars per day are required to qualify as being poor, nor how many poor people there are, nor how many more poor people we need to have before we collectively acknowledge the system is an outdated and broken one.

Poverty is not just a problem related only to low-income countries; it is also a problem for places such as the US and the UK, both home to many billionaires. The US alone in 2020 was home to over 500 billionaires.[32]

Hunger, starvation and undernourishment

The level of poverty correlates to the level of hunger, starvation and undernourishment. Our current situation, as shown in these UN facts and figures on hunger, speaks for itself:

- An estimated 2 billion people in the world did not have regular access to safe, nutritious and sufficient food in 2019.
- If recent trends continue, the number of people affected by hunger will surpass 840 million by 2030, or 9.8 percent of the global population.
- 144 million children under age 5 were affected by stunting in 2019, with three quarters living in Southern Asia and sub-Saharan Africa.[33]

Health

Let's look at some key facts from common diseases.

Malaria: A preventable and curable disease transmitted by the bite of an infected Anopheles mosquito. The estimated number of malaria deaths was 627,000 in 2020. Of those, 476,520 children under 5 years died in Africa (96% of all Malaria deaths were in Africa, and 80% were children under 5 years).

Imagine how the inhabitants of Europe or Australia would react if in a single year over 400,000 kids under 5 years of age died of a preventable and curable disease such as Malaria.

Influenza: The annual epidemics are estimated to result in about 3 to 5 million cases of severe illness, and about 290,000 to 650,000 respiratory deaths.[34]

Cholera: An acute diarrheal infection caused by eating or drinking

32 K Raworth op. cit.; Forbes https://www.forbes.com/billionaires/
33 United Nations, Facts and Figures Hunger: https://www.un.org/sustainabledevelopment/hunger/
34 World Health Organisation, Influenza (seasonal) https://www.who.int/news-room/fact-sheets/detail/influenza-(seasonal)

food or water contaminated with the bacterium vibrio cholerae. Children and adults can die within hours if untreated. Although 21,000 to 143,000 deaths worldwide may be considered low, this disease and its numbers are likely to rise, with more outbreaks in the years to come. Provision of safe water and sanitation is critical to controlling cholera outbreaks.[35]

A warmer planet brings problems of water resources and food availability and – considering global poverty levels, rising sea levels and the increasing number of people displaced by both conflict and climate change – creates conditions for different infectious diseases to spread. Indeed, as the Intergovernmental Panel on Climate Change's Special Report: Global Warming of 1.5 degrees notes, these factors will likely lead to an increase in the number of cases for diseases such as malaria and dengue fever.[36]

It will not be surprising that new infectious viral diseases such as COVID-19 continue to affect us in the future, as we are already seeing with its different deadly variants.

It is essential to properly invest in our public health systems and support the wellbeing of our communities worldwide. The effect of not doing this have been clearly seen in the current pandemic. The effects of COVID-19 in what we consider "developed" societies is catastrophic.

For instance, before the start of December 2020, the US alone had over 250,000 deaths due to COVID-19. In less than a year, they had more deaths than the approximate casualties from the 10 years of war in Vietnam. By early February 2021, there were over 450,000 casualties, more than the second world war. By mid-August that same year, there were over 630,000. By mid-December, it was 820,000, and by July 2022, over 1,000,000.

In contrast, the leadership of some countries in tackling COVID-19 has been shown in lower casualty rates.

Indeed, among others, the Nordic countries, as well as Vietnam,

---

35 World Health organization, Cholera – Key facts https://www.who.int/news-room/fact-sheets/detail/cholera
36 Intergovernmental Panel on Climate change (IPCC), 2018: Summary for Policymakers. In: Global Warming of 1.5°C. An IPCC Special Report on the impacts of global warming of 1.5°C above pre-industrial levels and related global greenhouse gas emission pathways, in the context of strengthening the global response to the threat of climate change, sustainable development, and efforts to eradicate poverty / Projected Climate Change, Potential Impacts and Associated Risks (B.5.2) [Masson-Delmotte, V., P. Zhai, H.-O. Pörtner, D. Roberts, J. Skea, P.R. Shukla, A. Pirani, W. Moufouma-Okia, C. Péan, R. Pidcock, S. Connors, J.B.R. Matthews, Y. Chen, X. Zhou, M.I. Gomis, E. Lonnoy, T. Maycock, M. Tignor, and T. Waterfield (eds.)]. In Press https://www.ipcc.ch/sr15/chapter/spm/

China, Taiwan, Cuba, El Salvador, Costa Rica, New Zealand and Australia, effectively adopted social and economic measures to deal with the pandemic following scientist, medical and other professional advice. It's not over yet though.

Perhaps, we could stop blaming China for the pandemic and take accountability for our own shortcomings. The no ratification of ICESCR, lack of its progressive implementation and hence disregard for this fundamental human rights convention, have played and continue to play a decisive role in our current reality.

The globalisation of the world economy and the neoliberal approach with privatisation as a key component have often diminished the provision of public services. One does not have to be an economist to know that government provide public services, they do so because of their public function and the fact that they are or should be for the benefit of their people – or at least that's what democracy should be about.

In contrast, when the public service is provided by the private sector, the benefits are for the shareholders, not society as a whole – despite the efforts of neoliberalists to argue that it will provide greater benefits to all because of the good and efficient administration. The real purpose is to generate profits for the shareholders. This weakens the provision of essential public services such as health services.[37]

Internally displaced people

IDPs and refugees worldwide will also be a catalyst for not just social upheaval, but the cause of more conflict and wars (as we are currently seeing).

In 2015, we had 65.3 million forcibly displaced worldwide[38]. By January 2019, this number had increased to 68.5 million, then 79.5 million in July 2020, 82.4 million in June 2021, and as of June 2022, 89.3 million.[39]

It is not being fatalistic, but realistic. It is a wake-up call for the imperative need to effectively put in place a system that tackles our global challenges.

37 B Svedberg, C Chinkin, G Mlinarevic, J True, M Rees and N P Isakovic 'A Feminist Perspective on Post-Conflict Restructuring and Recovery – the Study of Bosnia and Herzegovina, Women's International League for Peace and Freedom (2017) (6)-(7).
38 Office of the United Nations High Commissioner for Refugees, Trends at a glance – 2015 in review: https://www.unhcr.org/576408cd7
39 Office of the United Nations High Commissioner for Refugees, Figures at a glance: https://www.unhcr.org/figures-at-a-glance.html

More than ever, the voices of those who discriminate, believe themselves superior and create more divisiveness and radicalisation should be neither supported nor amplified.

Questioning our beliefs and understandings must be done not just because is the moral thing to do, nor even because is the right thing to do, but because our existence as a species depends on it.

We are at a point of history that if we continue with our discriminatory mentality, practices and approaches, our species, as is happening to hundreds of other species, will most likely perish.

Saving the planet or saving ourselves?

There is a general assumption about the need to 'save' the planet. We believe we are the masters of this planet, and due to the risk of climate change, we need to save it.

But the planet will go on without us; it looks after itself.

We don't need to save planet Earth; we need to save ourselves.

However, to do that, we need to let go of our individualistic worldviews and perhaps go back to what Indigenous communities around the world know. That we are part of nature, part of the ecosystems.

The sooner we realise this, the sooner we will start appreciating the uniqueness and pricelessness of the living organisms, species and ecosystems that coexist on this "tiny little blue speck of dust" we call planet Earth – and start effectively addressing the global challenges our species has created.

Yes, I am one of those also worried about what sort of world we will leave for Keith Richards when we die…

But seriously, some of us may not be into saving ourselves or saving our species. Perhaps we may feel so attached and committed to our corporate careers and worldviews that our whole identities, perspectives and lives are intertwined with the corporation. I was almost one of them while living in Colombia, and many of our government leaders are. Or maybe we have given up having faith in our species. Who can blame us? We can cause a lot of harm by action or inaction. Testament to this are the figures in the Discrimination section above.

But the need for climate action is paramount. If it is not for us, our children and future generations, perhaps maybe some of us may do it for the places that are disappearing, like the Great Barrier Reef, or threatened species like polar bears, Andean bears, koalas, the platypus, bald eagles, Andean condors, the roadrunner-like Banded Ground-Cucko, or the Rufous Hummingbird just to name a few.

There are over 800 endangered species just in Colombia[40], including species from the biological groups of plants, coral jellyfish and sea anemones, amphibians, birds, reptiles, mammals, fish, insects, and crustaceans.

These numbers also exemplify the level of ecological degradation we have allowed on our planet. But if they're still not enough to convince us, we could think of the nearly 3 billion (3,000,000,000) animals killed or displaced only in the Australian fires of 2019–2020.

Maybe watching My Octopus Teacher or its parody My Kreepy Teacher has highlighted the feeling that we do not really know much of the natural world, and perhaps want to feel and experience a greater connection with nature. Indeed, developing greater respect, understanding and compassion for the animal kingdom also relates to the reduction of GHG emissions, as we'll see below.

Dr Jane Goodall's work has shown us the importance of the animal kingdom. Her reflections on World Animal Day are definitely worth checking out.[41] As Dr Goodall puts it, "we are part and not separate from the animal kingdom." And by this I'm sure she isn't just referring to the 98.6% of DNA we share with a chimpanzee. It is that they too have emotions, they love, they are compassionate, and show behaviour we may consider as good and bad – and that we are basically chimps.

Feeling fear and pain and having personalities and intelligence is indeed all over the animal kingdom. This includes the great apes, elephants, dolphins, birds, cows, pigs, crows, and of course our octopus friend with nine brains, one in the head and one in each arm, and who is amazingly creative when it comes to problem-solving.

There is always hope to bring more awareness to create change for a sustainable planet. What we are trying to achieve is to protect ourselves from extinction, and that would require caring for the land and the diverse ecosystems and species that inhabit the Earth.

---

40 Earths Endangered Creatures, Endangered Species Search by Area selection:
http://www.earthsendangered.com/search-regions3.asp?mp=1&search=1&sgroup=allgroups&ID=92
41 J Goodall 'Remarks for World Animal Day 2020' 4 October 2020, available at
https://www.youtube.com/watch?v=9le192CyzYY

Our carbon footprint

Climate change is caused by human-induced Green House Gas (GHG) emissions. It is exacerbated by our economic and political system that keeps supporting the fossil fuel industry, and the seeming need for the economy to grow. More on this later.

It is also becoming common knowledge that to avoid ecological and societal collapse, our ability to adapt and mitigate the effects of climate change requires the effective reduction of GHG emissions.

The global ecological footprint has already exceeded earth's capacity. We need 5 planets for everyone in the world to live like an Australian or Kuwaiti, and about 4 planets to live like they do in Sweden, Canada and the USA.[42]

In the documentary Fight for Planet A: Our Climate Challenge by the Australian Broadcasting Corporation, a series of three episodes shows the importance of addressing climate change, and that not only governments and corporations have to pay the price of GHG emissions.

Seeing the Australian droughts, floods and fires, people are already paying the price, and there is no question we'll continue to do so in the decades to come if our species is still here. Hence, we must also be part of the solution in reducing our individual and family GHG emissions.

For those who haven't watched the series, in one of the episodes, the host of the program puts 6 and a half tonnes of ice in a public square and begins asking people how long it would take for an average Australian with their carbon emissions to melt the blocks. Some said 12 months, 6 months; I think someone almost terrified said one month. It turned out that for an average fellow Aussie it takes 10 days. In other words, the carbon emissions of every one of us in Australia on average melt 6 and half tonnes of ice every 10 days.

I was terrified, and so was every single one of the people interviewed. One suggested speaking to the Prime Minister of Australia. The host tried to do so in one episode, only to see the then Prime Minister Mr Scott Morrison literally running away from him.[43]

I wish like billions of people around the world that the effects of climate change would disappear by denying climate change exists, by not talking about it, or by trying to run away from its effects. But they won't.

---

[42] K Raworth op. cit. p 217
[43] Australian Broadcasting Corporation 'Fight for Planet A: Our Climate Challenge' Aug 16, 2020

Many would agree on the need to put pressure on governments to make policies that make electric cars accessible to most of the population. That it may not be about giving car manufacturers billions of dollars in subsidies and tax exemptions, as we continue to give to the fossil fuel industry (yes, billions. Billions that could be used to comply with ICESCR).

I think though that we may have already passed this point. What needs to be taken is a real and not a tokenistic approach to tackling climate change.

We urgently need to tackle our transport system emissions. We need a worldwide policy whereby cars built to use and burn fossil fuels are no longer allowed. In other words, car manufacturers should only be allowed to produce electric cars.

Only in the last decade (2010–2019) the estimated worldwide automobile production was 890 million vehicles. That is an average of 89 million vehicles per year. In the years 2017, 2018 and 2019, the estimated production was 97, 97 and 92 million respectively.[44]

Imagine the number of vehicles produced before 2010 that are on the roads burning fossil fuels worldwide. We do not have to be mathematicians. There are billions of vehicles on the planet burning fossil fuels every minute, every day, 7 days a week.

If we are to reduce GHG emissions to save our species, this is the type of policy required. It also needs to establish a timeframe whereby cars that burn fossil fuels need to be replaced by electric ones.

Of course, anything that could be done to reduce our GHG emissions should be pursued. For example, we could be more supportive of local producers to reduce emissions from transporting goods. (This consideration may not apply once we have trucks, planes, and other means of transport that do not require fossil fuels.) We could also continue looking at our consumption of meat, which creates large amounts of GHG.

However, while these actions are important, they're not as urgent as our transport emissions. Beef production, for example, represents less than 15% of all human-induced emissions.[45] We really need to prioritise reducing the emissions created by transport.

---

[44] https://www.statista.com/statistics/262747/worldwide-automobile-production-since-2000/
[45] Food and Agriculture Organization of the United Nations (FAO) 'Tackling Climate Change through Livestock, A Global Assessment of Emissions and Mitigation Opportunities' (FAO 2013) p14

Waste food also creates large amounts of GHG. In Colombia, Mum would never waste food. What we didn't eat one day, we would eat at the next meal in a different form, and if that wasn't eaten, a soup would then be made. We always ended up eating it, so leftovers were not wasted. We still tease her about it.

Both my parents reminded us often that there were millions of people malnourished and dying of starvation worldwide. That was a fact that is still sadly the case. When I throw out leftovers, I can't help but think of the estimated 2 billion people (2,000,000,000 human beings) who did not have regular access to safe, nutritious and sufficient food in 2019, and that one in ten people in the world are exposed to severe levels of food insecurity.[46]

We could all try harder not to waste food (my apologies to those who already also love a good *calentado* – that's the leftovers from the previous night with a few more ingredients added, including veggies, with a fried egg on top). More people could use leftovers more often to create their own omelettes, tortillas, burgers, tacos or pasta.

This is something simple we could all do more of. It is the classic win-win scenario, wasting no food, saving money, having a tasty, easy and quick meal to cook for lunch or dinner next day, while reducing GHG emissions.

Waiting for a saviour while living in the binary

In our western world there is the idea, reinforced by Hollywood, that someone wearing a uniform is going to save us. Different authors have spoken about this, including Oxford scholar and bestselling author Yuval Noah Harari in his trilogy.[47]

The common depictions of men saving the world reinforce the patriarchal ideas of power, dominance and use of force so embedded in our socio-economic and political structures and beliefs.

With all due respect to the military, and although the military of course has its place on our planet, it is unlikely anyone wearing uniform will save us from our current global challenges.

Some may not be convinced of the need for the demilitarisation of our global economy, and that there is a need to keep the military and

---

[46] United Nations, Facts and Figures Hunger: https://www.un.org/sustainabledevelopment/hunger/
[47] Y N Harari 'Homo Deus, A Brief History of Tomorrow' (Penguin Random House UK 2017); 'Sapiens, A Brief History of Humankind' (Penguin Random House UK 2015); '21 Lessons for the 21st Century' (Jonathan Cape London 2018)

its budgets. We may, however, transform the military in the future – the scenario below could perhaps only be a possibility when non-discrimination is a cultural norm respected by our species.

Imagine that instead of producing more weapons and going to war to "set countries free" through more violence (which continues to happen in countries where high levels of inequality and extreme poverty exist), we could reach an agreement whereby the military is redefined.

The new "military" personnel could go to the most impoverished, neglected regions, countries and cities of our planet in partnership with the local communities to build solar and wind farms, schools, libraries, hospitals, houses, universities, parks and roads.

The premise is simple. Instead of going to combat, to fight, to destroy, to dominate, the new military are deployed only to build, to construct, to repair. I know that for some, the above may sound like a naïve proposition, but the military personnel in many countries already act in different capacities other than fighting or providing security.

The military currently provides humanitarian assistance and disaster relief in response to the effects of climate change. For instance, the Australian Defence Force has been deployed to respond to floods, cyclones and bushfires using logistics, communications and engineering assistance to transport and evacuate people, deliver food and water to communities, build temporary shelters and support firefighting efforts.[48]

Considering the more frequent and tragic weather events, including the regular and longer fires in so many parts of the world like the USA, Australia, Europe, it appears the military will continue to act in the capacity described.

The idea of the military as saviours correlates with the current path of militarisation and securitisation of the global economy. And it is very concerning. This increasing militarisation of our world can clearly be seen in the military budgets – according to the figures provided by the Stockholm International Peace Research Institute (SIPRI), global military spending reached \$1,917 billion in 2019. The five largest

---

[48] Royal Commission into National Natural Disaster Arrangements Report 28 Oct 2020 (187 – 192) https://naturaldisaster.royalcommission.gov.au/publications/royal-commission-national-natural-disaster-arrangements-report

spenders were the US, China, India, Russia and Saudi Arabia.[49]

The obsolete idea that peace can be achieved through physical, military means is something that we must continue to challenge. Indeed, stopping militarisation and reducing the military budgets and redistributing these resources to address local and global inequalities should be a priority.

The answer to what is required is seemingly clear, but it raises a conundrum. War is a business, and as a business, it has been, is, and will be protected by those who benefit from human suffering.

The five permanent members of the United Nations Security Council – China, France, Russia, the United Kingdom and the USA – are also the main exporters of weapons. And as mentioned, the USA, China and Russia are the largest spenders on military budgets.

Thus, it is a simple matter of logic, with the amount of money destined to the military, we will continue to create more conflict and wars worldwide. And given that many private corporations, including the ones in the business of extracting natural resources, also "benefit" from the global militarisation and securitisation agenda, it appears they are so far not inclined to change their profitable economic activities.

The UN Security Council has the primary responsibility of the maintenance of international peace and security, and in performing these duties, it shall act according to the Purposes and Principles of the United Nations.[50] However, if we keep believing that we can achieve peace through military means, the chances of living in a more peaceful world will continue to be only an illusion.

A profound change needs to occur, not only within the United Nations and the members of the UN Security Council, but culturally, a switch of consciousness. Education in this regard is paramount.

We do need to change, and the way societies evolve and survive is by questioning and challenging the status quo, especially if the answers and the practices we continue to apply deepen the issues.

It is not paranoia; we have been programmed to accept conflict and war as inherent in the human condition and as an integral part of our societies.

The influence of corporations covering news, media, movies, children's programs, toys, video games, to name a few, keep the

---

[49] Stockholm International Peace Research Institute (SIPRI) https://www.sipri.org/media/press-release/2020/global-military-expenditure-sees-largest-annual-increase-decade-says-sipri-reaching-1917-billion
[50] United Nations Charter (1945) Article 23, 24 (1)-(2)

message of patriarchal, gender stereotypes, and war and conflict as natural, something unavoidable and alive – militarisation is indeed a socio-political process.[51]

The conditioning and ongoing indoctrination of gender role stereotypes can be seen for instance in Israel, where military service is compulsory and gender roles are predefined. The role of mothers, for example, is to worry about and focus on the need to support their soldier sons. Girls are also indoctrinated with the commitment to country and prepared for service roles within the military. Following patriarchal attitudes, they are also encouraged to find a husband.

As Israeli peace activist and mother Ruth Hiller writes, "As parents we strengthen the belief that 'duty calls' and that heroism in the name of Israel is the highest aspiration. We all identify with the role of the warrior and the use of violence to solve the problem... We convince ourselves, and in turn our children, that we are in the midst of 'a war of no choice'".[52] This indoctrination occurs through different avenues, including commercial advertisements.

By the same token, the beliefs and understanding of conflict by Palestinian people may not greatly differ from Israeli people.

It is certainly up to us whether we start a new process within the "process of evolution", seeing the limitless opportunities of a non-militarised world where substantial gender equality and economic, social, and political inclusiveness constitute not only the legal but more importantly the cultural norm.

With the tense diplomatic relations between China and the USA, and whoever comes next after Biden and Harris, the international community needs to keep a close watch. Fighting might not only be around the negotiation of "Free Trade Agreements" but could escalate to catastrophic outcomes for humanity.

While we are waiting for the saviours, we have fixed in our brains a binary type of society, with anachronistic ideas of good vs bad, angels vs evil ones, and the most typical and perhaps most dangerous of all, them vs us.

As Stoknes argues in What We Think About When We Try Not to Think About Global Warming, "the division between the 'righteous us' and the 'evil them' is widespread in western culture after 2000 years

---

[51] C Enloe 'Understanding militarism, militarisation, and the linkages with globalisation' Using a Feminist Curiosity, in Gender and Militarism Analysing the Links to Strategize for Peace (2014) (7).

[52] R Hiller 'Militarised parenthood in Israel (Women Peacemakers Program [wpm] 2014) 59, 60.

of Christianity… This assumption of moral opposition is mostly destructive, further entrenching polarization and fundamentalism, damaging the cohesion and cooperation necessary to tackle the problems we face."[53]

Refugees and people displaced by war and climate change

It is time to stop supporting the idea of going to war as the solution to set countries "free" or using the vague and empty phrases of pseudo-nationalist leaders – phrases like "our national interest," "to protect our values" and "to protect our way of life." Or, more recently, "to protect our economy."

It's time to stop using the false and obsolete understanding that physical, coercive, and military means will bring peace and stability to any region.

Using military means does not, has not and will not bring peace and stability.

This is not only clear from an academic perspective, but I have also known that at a personal level, having been born, raised and lived for 26 years in a country of conflict. I know violence, using force, physical means, and the anachronistic idea to dominate only creates more violence.

Violence reinvents itself in cycles when the roots of the problems are not tackled. Conflict and war are the result of not pursuing socially conscious and more egalitarian societies.

Indeed, problems of health and violence are more common in more unequal societies. Harvard professor Ichiro Kawachi described inequality as a "social pollutant." Thus, tackling inequality is about improving the psychosocial wellbeing of the whole society.[54]

It is a shame not only for governments, countries, political leaders, corporations and billionaires that continue to play the game of war, but also to us as a species to accept a socio-economic system that keeps investing billions of dollars in the industry of conflict and war. That supports and subsidises the fossil fuel industry and allows absurd levels of poverty, hunger and inequalities worldwide, and with a political system that treats refugees, asylum seekers and stateless people in many

---

[53] As quoted in R Huntley 'How to talk about Climate Change in a Way That Makes a Difference' (Murdock Books 2020) (126)

[54] K Pickett and R Wilkinson 'The Spirit Level Authors: Why Society is More Unequal Than Ever,' The Guardian 9 March 2014 https://www.theguardian.com/commentisfree/2014/mar/09/society-unequal-the-spirit-level; K Pickett and R Wilkinson 'The Spirit Level' (London penguin 2009)

ways worse than criminals.

Indeed, criminals at least have rights to some procedural guarantees and to receive a judgement. But we are treating refugees and people displaced by war and climate change as less than human when we should be offering them protection.

This not only dehumanises us more, it shows how we keep feeding a narrative that is full of lies by our socio-economic and political systems and accepted understandings. It is common that politicians in many countries worldwide treat refugees as a threat to society. They continue the binary narrative of them vs us, and the lies and inaccurate picture that some sectors of the media portray. Here in Australia, as happens in many parts of the world, it is not unusual to hear that others are "stealing our jobs," "causing violence" "damaging our society" and that "they need to adopt our values."

Any person that migrates to another country, whether a refugee, a person displaced by war or climate change, "an expat" or a migrant like me, wants to contribute to society, and the reality is most of us do. We do not want to be a burden.

It is illogical to use a false, dishonest narrative, creating more discrimination, racism and radicalisation for political gain while disregarding that most continents around the world, including Australia, the Americas and Europe, were built by the sweat and tears of migrants.

Let's look at the situation in Australia, according to the 2020 report on Australia's offshore processing policies by the Refugee Council of Australia.[55]

According to the report, on 19 July 2013, the Australian government announced that anyone who arrived by boat in Australia to seek protection and was taken to offshore processing centres on Nauru and Manus Island would never be resettled in Australia, even if found and recognised to be a refugee. The Australian government, in maintaining this cruel policy for over 7 years, spent $7.6 billion for just over 3,000 people. The government tried to justify this policy through saying that it saves lives and stops people from drowning at sea.

The report goes on to say that the offshore processing policy does not save lives, but rather means "we are killing people more slowly and

---

[55] Refugee Council of Australia: 'Seven years on: An Overview of Australia's Offshore Processing Policies' (July 2020) https://www.refugeecouncil.org.au/wp-content/uploads/2020/07/RCOA-Seven-Years-On.pdf

more remotely, starving them of hope, and denying them a future." Indeed, "Some were teenagers, arriving in Australia alone. They are now young men and women, their dreams for the future shattered, the most important years of their lives wasted while they were being shifted from one country to another, from one detention centre to another."

Perhaps some other of the report's key figures could also be helpful here: 4,183 people sent offshore since 13 August 2012; 942 returned to their country of origin; 227 still in Papua New Guinea (PNG); 209 still in Nauru; 2063 in Australia; 730 resettled in a third country; and 12 people who have died.

These figures do not include those born in offshore facilities:

"Between 19 July 2013 and 28 February 2019, 46 children were born to people transferred offshore who remained in Nauru, and 125 children were born to those transferred from Nauru to Australia. No official statistics have been released on the number of children born in PNG…". Due to the people's support of refugees and asylum seekers and the #KidsOffNauru campaign, however, on 28 February 2019, the last four children on Nauru thankfully departed.

It is time that we collectively start asking the right questions, particularly as others including the UK are considering our "enlightened" Australian approach. How much does it cost to build, operate and run jails/offshore detention centres? How much does it cost to maintain a regime so discriminatory? How much is spent per refugee in our inhumane system?

To say the offshore processing system is expensive is an understatement. As the report outlines, it costs more than $1 billion a year, according to the annual figures published by the Department of Home Affairs since 2013–2014. Since then, it says, the costs have totalled $7.618 billion. If we divide that total by 3,127, the total number of people taken to offshore facilities since 19 July 2013, that equates to $2.44 million per person.

And this does not even consider the fact that many of those people were returned or removed to their home countries, or resettled in a third country, well before the last financial year. If we consider that, the cost per person for many would be significantly higher.

The treatment of refugees and stateless people from many countries including Australia exemplifies not only that the unfair, unjustified and illegal treatment of refugees equals racism and discrimination, but that such treatment also appears to be a way for our corporate world to find another way "to do business."

Throughout COVID-19, we all have experienced difficulties in adapting and keeping a positive outlook. It's not only levels of unemployment that have gone up, mental health issues and domestic violence have also increased in most countries.

Many of us are very lucky to experience the isolation of this pandemic in the comfort of our homes and the company of some of our loved ones. Imagine those who have been displaced by war and climate change, those who are stateless, refugees and asylum seekers. The suffering and devastation that they have gone through is almost incomprehensible for most of us,[56] and a testament to the power of the human spirit.[57]

Most have struggled for years to get to a country that could welcome them; instead, we are putting some of them in detention centres (jails), in some cases for an indefinite time. In Australia, some refugee applicants have been in offshore detention centres for years waiting for the assessment of their situation – some up to 8 years. Of course, there should be a timeframe to process applications, but years?

Working with the international community in partnership with neighbouring countries to reduce the number of people jumping on boats and risking their lives to get to a safe country is essential. There is no excuse. Treating refugees and asylum seekers the way we do is not just illegal, it is inhumane. We have crossed the line, and we need to stop.

According to international obligations, a person who is a refugee by international law is entitled to claim protection from any of the 150 state parties to the refugee regime. Refugee status is not a status that is granted by states; it is simply recognised by them.[58] In other words, "he does not become a refugee because of recognition, but is recognised because he is a refugee."[59]

For most of us, doing the mental exercise of putting ourselves in

---

56 D Nyuol Vincent with C Nader 'The Boy Who Wouldn't Die' (Fairfax Books 2013)
57 Behrouz Boochani 'No Friend but The Mountains' (Picador 2018)
58 J. C. Hathaway & M Foster 'The Law of Refugee Status Second Edition' (Cambridge University Press 2014) (1-2); UNHCR, Handbook on Procedures and Criteria for Determining Refugee Status under the 1951 Convention and the 1967 Protocol relating to the Status of Refugees, UN Doc. HCR/IP/4/Eng/REV.3 (2011) ("Handbook"). At [28]; Refugee Convention, at Article 1(A) (2)
59 Hathaway and Foster op. cit. p 26

the shoes of someone else is simply too confronting. Perhaps it is also the legacy of our individualistic societies and approaches.

But let's try harder. Let's try to imagine only for a moment we were refugees: how would I feel if I hadn't committed any crime, and I was running away from my country due to the fear of being persecuted for my race, religion, nationality, membership of a particular social group or political opinion?[60] Risking my life, with the hope I find a safe place to live.

Instead, I am sent to a jail – a detention centre on a remote island. How would I feel if I were effectively being put in a state of limbo? I do not know why I am in jail, or under what charges. I have no idea when I will recover my freedom or which country will allow me to continue my life …

How would I react? How would I cope after not months but years of being in a prison without having committed any crime? What would I do?

I may feel I am powerless, and perhaps there is nothing I can do. Would I sign some papers and let them take me back to the country I am desperately running away from?

The reality is the protection of some of the most basic human rights simply does not apply to me…

The above description is the actual reality for too many fellow humans. If we understand our global challenges, the current worldwide reality means being displaced by conflict or climate change could also happen to us or our children. It is already happening to millions of fellow human beings.

How would you like or expect the country we may need to go to – or our children may need to go to – to treat us or them?

I hope, like millions of people worldwide, that our leaders could empathise and put themselves in the shoes of the forgotten ones.

Indigenous understandings – re-learning

Our common ancestors lived in tribes, working collectively with a close connection to and understandings of nature, land and their ecosystems. This is almost forgotten.

I have had the privilege of calling Australia home now for over two decades. The Australian Aboriginal nations' cultures, languages, traditions and resilience are something we can all be proud of.

---

[60] Convention Relating to the Status of Refugees 1951 Article 1, Definition of the term Refugee

Some Aboriginal Australians speak 2, 3, 4, 5 or 6 different Aboriginal languages, and on top of that, English. The cultural richness of Aboriginal nations is something we are really only now discovering.

The first peoples of Australia have been here from time immemorial. Science keeps evolving, making new discoveries, telling us that Aboriginals have been in Australia for over 65,000 years, but some archaeologist findings suggest Aboriginals have been here for over 125,000 years.[61]

Perhaps looking at these years it makes more sense when in context we see what we have done to our planet in terms of the devastation of nature and different ecosystems since the industrial revolution. Indeed, the industrial revolution took place less than 300 years ago, yet the Aboriginal nations in Australia lived in peace and in harmony with the environment and other nations for tens of thousands of years.

The massacres, slavery, exploitation and discrimination towards the Aboriginal nations since European settlement, as happened to most if not all Indigenous communities worldwide, are undeniable.

Also, Australian Aboriginal nations and indeed Indigenous populations all over the world for thousands of years have known about what we have now come to call sustainability. They have not only known about it, they have applied it daily, knowing to behave as part of and not separate from nature. Thus, the intimate connection with land and water sources, with Pachamama, Gaia, La Ñuke Mapu, Tatei Yurianaka, Papa, Papatūānuku, Ina Maka, Madre Tierra (Mother Earth).

This understanding has interesting ramifications that we all could learn from.

Collectively and philosophically, Indigenous communities are almost naturally looking for balance, finding equilibrium. Respecting the wisdom of elders as they pass on the knowledge and traditions that have seen them survive for thousands of years.

The individuals of Indigenous communities do not have property titles. They are custodians, protectors, caretakers of the land. After all, it is Mother Earth we are talking about. You do not own people; you do not own your mother.

Their decision-making process is not for a few to decide, it generally involves community, with everyone invited and listened to.

---

[61] M Langton Welcome to Country: A travel guide to Indigenous Australia (Hardie Grant Travel 2018) (1,6)

When a decision is made, it is generally made not only with consideration for the wellbeing of those currently alive as well as the next generation, but also several generations ahead, and always keeping in mind the legacy of their ancestors.

Some of the Indigenous wisdom perhaps resides in an intrinsic understanding that we humans as species are part of ecosystems, and as we continue manipulating and destroying the natural world and natural habitats, we eventually destroy ourselves.

Perhaps it is time we all have some humility and respect for our Aboriginal Nations and Indigenous communities worldwide and learn from them too. It is time for us to re-learn.

Furthermore, the members of Aboriginal Nations, the Traditional Custodians of the land we call Australia, were not nomads and hunter gatherers. They were not barbarians (savages) nor an inferior race, as European settlers and some of their future generations tried to make us believe.[62]

Many Aboriginal nations were agriculturalist, worked the land, built houses, cemeteries, canals. They had and have a vibrant fishery industry. They have traditions, an advanced knowledge of their environment, a unique connection with land and water resources, and a level of spirituality and consciousness that many Australians and the entire world continues to appreciate and learn from.

I recently read the book Dark Emu by writer Bruce Pascoe. Bruce is an Australian writer with Bunurong, Tasmanian and Yuin heritage, and a very inspiring human being.

On the 1st of October 2020, with the state of Victoria and its capital Melbourne in lockdown due to the COVID-19 pandemic, I had the opportunity through the University of Melbourne to see and hear Bruce speak about Australian Aboriginals over Zoom. I'd love to share some of his reflections.

As I've mentioned, to tackle our global challenges, we need to challenge our mindset and beliefs, and that includes the belief of Europeans descendants' superiority over the Aboriginal and Indigenous populations, as well as other "races" not only in Australia but worldwide. Bruce mentioned that in 120,000 years of Australian Aboriginal culture, there was never a war for taking the land, because

---

[62] B Pascoe Dark Emu (Magabala Books Aboriginal Corporation, Broome Western Australia. First published 2014)

that's against Aboriginal Law.

"War and human conflict is not a pre-condition of human beings," he said. "The earth is mother earth and cannot be stolen... It's time we love her."

He reflected also on the importance of Law, of generosity of spirit, of caring for people, land and country.

"The philosophical achievement of Australian Aboriginals where land cannot be owned is an opportunity to reflect upon and to be inspired, and behave socially, economically and spiritually along those values."

The reality of Australian Aboriginals and indeed, most of us in our current system, is to work our entire lives for the benefit of other families. Families that we never meet. It is something we need to confront.

Bruce confessed that it was an accident he wrote Dark Emu. He was checking on what the Aboriginals Elders were saying, so he started looking at historical records and the records of explorers. "I realised the massive fraud not only to our people (Aboriginals) but to Australians."

What Bruce mentioned next applies perhaps not only to Australian Aboriginals, but many diverse Indigenous nations and communities worldwide, minority groups, IDPs, refugees, asylum seekers and stateless people: "Embracing Aboriginals is to say no to racism, no to fracking. Not out of guilt and shame over Australian history, but because we want to have a genuine relationship."

Moreover, Indigenous self-determination and respect for Indigenous cultures, including cultural property rights, is needed. The challenges for instance that Indigenous people can have with recognition of cultural property rights when they relate to cultural loss are because culture is usually seen with a contemporary definition – as something that keeps changing, and hence some may argue, means damage or loss may not occur.[63]

Although it is not easy to balance the above, respect and recognition for Indigenous cultural property rights and an understanding of culture as evolving are not necessarily mutually exclusive. In very simple terms, culture can also be anything we consciously decide we want to create. That could mean going back to re-learn some of the understandings

---

[63] S Kirsch Engaged Anthropology, Politics Beyond the Text'(University of California Press 2018) 138, 139, 140, 141, 142

we used to have, and which many Indigenous communities worldwide have.

If I was asked to summarise how we might solve the cultural challenges I've outlined in this chapter, I would say it is about deleting discrimination from our vocabulary. Something we could also reflect upon is the understanding of the word democracy by the Wayu Indigenous in La Guajira in Colombia:

Democracia = La manera de valorar a todos (Democracy = The way to value everyone)

We could ask ourselves: Do our democracies as they currently operate value everyone?

The collective understandings, connection with nature and resilience of Indigenous communities worldwide is something that could be an inspiration to us all. As Chief Oren Lyons Jr, Faith Keeper of the Onondaga tribe of the Haudenosaunee (Iroquois) Nation asks:

"Who is speaking for the water of the earth? Who is speaking for the trees and the forests? Who is speaking for the fish – for the whales, for the beavers, for our children?" [64]

.

---

[64] D R Boyd The Rights of Nature: A Legal Revolution that Could Save the World (ECW Press 2017) Introduction xxi

4
SOCIAL CHALLENGES AND OPPORTUNITIES

The conditioning of our current socio-economic and political structures makes us think under the constraint of those.

It is common in both the "developed" and the "developing" world that any type of criticism of the capitalist system – including its evident shortcomings in the application of humanist values – is seen as left-wing, socialist or communist, and that this is therefore evil.

However, the need for a new reality must include a different path than the industrial revolution took us down in the past, with communist dictatorships, fascist ideologies that continue to "inspire" many countries (still camouflaged as "national values" or "our way of life"), and liberal democracies.[65]

Neither capitalism nor socialism

Addressing our global challenges should require us not to resurrect or continue these inapplicable and failed ideologies but rather inspire us as a species to think more creatively.

The challenge is not only to survive but thrive in a peaceful and sustainable way with our own species and learn to coexist with other species that inhabit and will inhabit this planet in the future.

Adopting a sustainable and collective approach is fundamental.

In the Nordic countries for instance, appropriate levels of funding and resources are put into housing, education, health, recreation and employment. And if one were to ask most Nordic citizens whether

---

[65] Y N Harari 'Homo Deus – A Brief History of Tomorrow', (Penguin Random House UK 2017) 461

they would consider themselves "socialists" most would say no.

If liberal democracies represent their constituents, the people, then that is precisely what a real democracy does and how it should look. In other words, compliance with ICESCR is what every citizen of any nation on our planet wants to see happening when they vote in democratic elections.

Evidence of this is what every political candidate in the world promises in election campaigns: more jobs, affordable housing, better hospitals, schools, roads, parks, education, health, etc. But no one calls it what that actually is, which is the application of ICESCR. Instead, we like to call it development, or social policies.

If you haven't read the International Covenant on Economic, Social and Cultural Rights[66], I implore you to do so. There is a stigma that if we bring the world inequalities or if we spell out ICESCR, God forbid, that is socialism. It is not.

It seems not only in Australia but in many countries, some of us have the misconception that if you believe in human rights, social justice and equality, you must be a socialist, a left-wing supporter, a hippy, or a combination of all three — and for some, that's certainly not viewed as the holy trinity.

However, effectively protecting and promoting fundamental human rights, as well as working for more socially conscious and egalitarian societies is simply what democratic, civilised and developed societies do.

Indeed, if you believe in your right of self-determination and to freely pursue your economic, social and cultural development, or that everyone has the right to just conditions of work, including fair wages and equal remuneration for work of equal value without distinction, or to have a decent living for you and your family, with safe and healthy working conditions as well as rest, leisure and reasonable limitations on working hours and periodic holidays with pay, or if you believe in the right to access social security, or share the understanding that the family is the natural and fundamental unit of society and therefore requires the widest protection and assistance, with special protection to mothers during a reasonable period before and after childbirth, including paid leave or leave with appropriate social security, or you agree in the right of everyone to an appropriate standard of living,

---

[66] International Covenant on Economic, Social and Cultural Rights, opened for signature 16 December 1966, 993 UNTS 3 https://www.ohchr.org/en/professionalinterest/pages/cescr.aspx

including adequate food, clothing and housing, or you recognise your right to enjoy the highest attainable standard of physical and mental health, and that regardless of where you were born or live, that countries need to work on the healthy development of the child and reducing infant mortality as well as improving all aspects of environmental and industrial hygiene and the prevention, treatment and control of epidemic, endemic, occupational and other diseases, and the creation of conditions that guarantee all medical service and attention in the event of sickness, or in the importance of everyone's right to education, to take part in cultural life, to enjoy the benefits of scientific progress and its applications, and also to protect the moral and material rights of any scientific, literary or artistic production you create, as well as the concept of international cooperation in the scientific and cultural fields, then believe in the importance of ICESCR.

Indeed, if you find yourself nodding to some if not all the points above, I'm sure you'd agree it doesn't mean you're a socialist. In fact, I think anyone reading the above would consider all of them pretty obvious things we just expect – basic markers of a decent life, regardless of how we might approach discussions of being on the left or right side of politics, or concepts like capitalism versus socialism.

Our current system, which tends to align with the concepts of neoliberal capitalism, is obsolete. It does not address the needs of our current societies and is clearly disregarding the bounds of our planet's capacity. More confrontingly, in many of our democratic countries, instead of effectively addressing our challenges, we have opted for more authoritarian types of governments.

The consequence is that, as happened in communist dictatorships of the past, knowledge and power are centralised, fundamental human rights are restricted, and the decisions benefit only a minority group, hence deepening the global challenges.

Unemployment and artificial intelligence (AI)

Higher levels of unemployment worldwide will continue to rise because of automation and developments in AI.

From the human rights perspective this scenario is at the core of human rights, the respect for the dignity of human beings. The right to work, and the right to an adequate standard of living, is being affected and will continue to be affected.

The two giants in the world of search engines and social networks,

Google and Facebook, use artificial intelligence (AI), algorithms, and due to their duopoly in the market, to some extent are already creating unemployment.

The use of AI has allowed them to produce more revenue than traditional advertising companies. The difference is substantial, to produce $10 million in revenue, both giants only require less than 10 employees each, whereas a public relations company, for example, might require over a hundred employees to generate the same revenue.[67]

Any business that advertises their products or services could do it through Facebook and Google ads, directly targeting those who may need or benefit from their products and services.

The challenge of AI as described by historian Yuval Noah Harari[68] is the potential of robots taking over the workforce in many industries for lower-skill jobs. This can create more inequalities and higher levels of unemployment. It is already happening, as we all know as we see it every day with the declining number of cashiers in brick-and-mortar enterprises like supermarkets. There is potential for this to be extended in the future to the skilled workforce, including general practitioners, lawyers, architects, accountants, and also drivers of machines, including cars, boats, planes or whatever means of transport robots would likely create and drive.

Yes, that robots would create. The Research and Development sector keeps developing and its machine learning keeps developing too.

One example that Harari refers to is the significant achievement by Google's Alpha Zero, a chess engine program developed in 4 hours through playing against itself without learning anything from human experience but rather by following machine-learning principles.

Alpha Zero defeated Stockfish, another chess engine that was built to include hundreds of years of human experience, including the seemingly wining moves of the likes of Gasparov, Lasker, Capablanca and Fisher. Out of 100 games, AlphaZero drew seventy-two and won twenty-eight.

AI is moving fast. It is quite unlikely that major regulatory interventions would take place, or if they do, whether that would make

---

[67] S Galloway 'Why Amazon, Apple, Facebook and Google Need to be Disrupted' Feb 8, 2018, https://www.esquire.com/news-politics/a15895746/bust-big-tech-silicon-valley/
[68] in Y N Harari '21 Lessons for the 21st Century' (Jonathan Cape 2018) Part I and II.

any impact. This is because of the uncertainty of new scenarios and the difficulties at international and domestic levels of legislation around these to be effectively enforced.

Corruption

For those who still want to believe that fighting is in our DNA, perhaps we could focus on channelling our fighting and warrior spirits to fight to end corruption.

I am one of those ready to channel my Indigenous Pijao ancestors, not with weapons but rather with logic and reasoning.

Corruption is everywhere and affects all of us. "At least $18.5 trillion is hidden by wealthy residents in tax havens … that money could end extreme income poverty twice over."[69]

Yes, twice.

The scandals of Panama and Paradise Papers may ring bells, as well as the names of members of royal families, politicians, businesspeople, and celebrities involved.

It is the greediness of our socio-economic system, and an education that promotes the accumulation of wealth, where happiness is attached to keep buying more properties, goods and services, without ethical, environmental and logical considerations.

The result is knowing that we the individuals of the Homo "Sapiens" species hide money in what we have called tax havens to avoid paying our share, when there are millions of people living in extreme poverty, dying of starvation and of preventable and curable diseases.

A new education in a different system where ethical and sustainable considerations are shaped from our homes and throughout the different stages of education is obviously needed.

Our current socio-economic system does not really care whether you have values or ethics.

It seems, you only have value if you can contribute to bringing, creating or supporting more wealth. It does not matter if you must step on others to achieve it – in fact, it encourages you to do so as it is all about competitiveness and who can bring more profits and sooner.

Businesses and even government agencies continue to cut many jobs, put many of their staff in unstable, casual, part-time hours, while

---

[69] K Raworth op. cit. p 235

paying their executives millions of dollars in bonuses and shares, as well as compensation when they leave their companies. This needs to change.

The billions we give and continue to give to the fossil fuel industries, with their lobby apparatus, are also part of our corrupted, symbiotic business and political culture.

In our current reality, it does not matter who wins in most democratic elections all over the world, because not only the fossil fuel industry but most corporations (as a common "business policy") donate to different political party candidates.

Thus, whether it's Australia with our Liberal and Labor political parties, the U.S with their Democrats and Republicans, or Britain with Conservative and Labour, it simply does not seem to make any substantial difference who wins the elections.

The governments of these three countries as examples (because the same happens in most countries) increasingly tend not to act for the benefit of their constituents, but rather corporations. This is evident not only in the amount of subsidies and tax exceptions but also in the levels of discrimination and the ecological degradation our planet carries.

I remember that before he was elected president of the U.S., Trump, while debating with other candidates including Hillary Clinton, said the system was broken. He publicly admitted that he had donated to political parties and that he called them 2–3 years later to ask for favours. Despite this public confession, his lack of ethics in both business and politics, and his misogynistic and racist approaches, he was elected.

More broadly, corporations and wealthy individuals right now can donate as they see fit in "democratic" general elections in most countries worldwide.

Surveillance capitalism

There has been a rise in what is being called surveillance capitalism[70], while our species keeps moving towards a digital economy.

The implication of data collection versus our rights to privacy, as well as freedom of speech versus hate speech, and allowing companies through fake news and false advertisements to influence elections, has

---

[70] Z Shosana 'The Age of Surveillance Capitalism' (New York: Public Affairs 2019) Chapter 18

not only supported extreme right-wing groups, but contributed to many of them rising to power.

At the core of the business of the two most influential companies at the vanguard of artificial intelligence – Google and Facebook – is the collection of data.

Originally, their business model was the use of the data we give them to be used or sold to third parties for marketing purposes. In this original scenario, the use of AI didn't pose many concerns except for the obvious right to privacy.

However, in the new reality of surveillance capitalism, traditional economic concepts such as the invisible hand in the market simply do not apply.

The hand is very visible, as an engineer from Facebook mentioned: "we are trying to map out everything in the world and how it relates to each other."

And as Eric Smichdt from Google mentioned, "You give us more information about you, about your friends, and we can improve the quality of your searches… we know where you are. We know where you've been. We can more or less know what you are thinking about."

Despite the legal and moral repercussions that hate speech, fake news and systemic disinformation have, and how they affect fundamental human rights, Facebook's position was clear. As long as content keeps growing the business and making it more profitable, that's what matters.

In the case of using social media to disseminate hate speech, the potential violation of fundamental human rights is clear. It involves the violation of legislation that promotes racial and religious tolerance, which is at the core of most human rights instruments.

In addition, hate speech promotes and creates violence not only in the online domain but it can translate to physical spheres. It has affected people's right to life and continues to be a clear cause of compromising such a fundamental right.

Moreover, the "development" of these two companies has brought questions not only about human rights compliance or moral standards that corporations should display, but the concerning trend towards the reduction of human beings as merchandise. We became the product.

What originally began as collecting data to sell us products according to our desires, emotions and likes, has changed. They not only now know our behaviour, they are predicting it – and more confrontingly perhaps, shaping it.

To be fair though, cinema, television and radio have also done this since they were introduced. However, in the case of fake news, what is at stake is not just human rights but democratic values and democracy itself, or whatever is left of it.

The disinformation campaigns allowed by Facebook in the 2016 U.S. election and the Brexit vote in the UK are not only problem of the UK and the U.S. alone. They have also been allowed in other countries including Indonesia, the Philippines, Australia, Brazil, Colombia, Germany, Spain and Ukraine.[71]

After European and U.S. politicians demanded answers from Google and Facebook for weakening democracy, and brands suspended their ads, both companies made public apologies – yet we are still waiting to see Google and Facebook's redefined values, levels of transparency and accountability, and more on the role they would play in addressing our global challenges.[72]

Given the power of corporations and the fact that both human rights as well as artificial intelligence are instruments that keep evolving, efforts directed to create binding agreements are important.

Perhaps agreements that include a type of governance that takes characteristics of the experimentalist governance, including open participation of relevant entities without hierarchies in decision-making; the elaboration by local actors who understand the context; and implementation of monitoring and reporting mechanisms[73]. This seems to be an interesting approach to keep exploring.

To trust that corporations are going to voluntarily self-regulate and create appropriate mechanisms to comply and adopt human rights standards and approaches as part of their values and policies seems naïve at best.

In the end, it seems it would be up to us, as members of civil society, whether we allow governments to continue not to take decisive action and continue to allow corporations to keep acting without proper accountability.

Perhaps billionaires may start seeing beyond the stock exchange, and the countries they currently call home. Our challenges will not be "fixed" under the current socio-political and economic system that

---

[71] Ibid Chapter 18, p 508
[72] Ibid Chapter 18, p 508
[73] D Grainne, R Keohanne and C Sabel 'New Modes of Pluralist Governance' (NYU Journal of International Law and Politics 45 [1] [726, 749,750, 751,752, 753,754, 756, 757, 758, 761, 762, 779, 780]

keeps believing a more militarised, authoritarian type of ruling will solve the problems.

Government leaders need to be better informed, more conscious about our global challenges and to start acting beyond the influence of corporations, because what we are facing is not some science fiction movie, but a harsh reality that cannot be solved by our current understandings.

Divide and rule – The domain of the fourth estate

The influence of media and the need to have more effective regulations is seen in the rise of Keith Rupert Murdoch's empire. The Australian of Scottish ancestry started off with a newspaper in Adelaide, Australia, and over 50 years, has managed to create a global media empire.

Mr Murdoch's influence is not only with his newspapers and media companies in Australia, but also the UK and the U.S.

His support of what we've historically called right-wing views is a secret to no-one. Throughout the years, he has formed an unholy alliance of the media with the fossil fuel industries. Evidence of this is his position, and position of many of his media companies throughout the years, of denying the existence of climate change.

The level of intervention, however, is not only in the denial of global threats. Mr Murdoch and his media empire have been big influencers if not determinants in general elections in Australia, the UK and the U.S.

The corruption within the media industry was made public in England when it was proven that some of his companies were hacking phones and computers. On top of that, their actions included bribes and coercion, thus looking like anything but the actions of a respected, reputable business.

The public enquiries and the court cases initiated by people who suffered these despicable acts affected Mr Murdoch's reputation and some of his pocket money, with hundreds of millions in compensation for damages caused.

Ironically, these court cases, although they affected him and his family, seemingly did not make him change his approaches and beliefs. Some may argue they worsened them. It is difficult to argue with those who have that view when we see that Fox "News" not only gave Trump the platform to become president of the United States but also a channel for Donald to keep perpetuating divisiveness and radicalisation.

It appears Mr Murdoch is a firm believer of the maxim "divide and rule" while many of us are still wondering what happened to transparent, independent, objective media news?

.

5
ECONOMIC CHALLENGES AND OPPORTUNITIES

The different cultural, social and economic challenges we are facing do not apply in isolation. They are all interconnected, and it is important to see them all as part of one bigger picture.

Our financial and economic system is broken.

To try to redefine our economic system, we must consider and effectively tackle the cultural and social challenges described in the previous chapter.

If we are to survive the climate crisis, our financial sector with their creation of money, as well as people's retirement funds and our savings, need to be distanced from military, security, weapons and fossil-fuel industry investments.

Otherwise, it will continue to be symbolic talk of a greener, fairer, and more sustainable world, while our species keeps falling apart on a path to self-destruction.

Looking at the figures mentioned in the cultural and discrimination sections in an earlier chapter, the numbers of forcibly displaced people in the refugees section, the figures in the social section, and particularly the billions hidden in tax havens as mentioned under corruption, it is clear our economic system is not just obsolete, it is broken.

We need a redefinition of our economic system.

In addition to the cultural and social considerations, the points outlined below could also be considered.

Free market the answer to our prayers?

Most if not all economists would probably agree that there is no such a thing as a free market. I wish politicians would stop saying there is a free market, or that "the free market" is the answer to our socio-economic problems.

To exemplify this, we only need to have a look at any "Free Trade Agreement." It is actually a joke that we call it "free." Every trade agreement is full of clauses that show the power and interest of diverse industries, including corporations that through lobbying make sure their interest is protected.

It is not about a "free market" without regulations, rather what and how we regulate, and perhaps more importantly, that for whatever regulations put in place, we make sure they are socially responsible, sustainable and widely culturally accepted.

Every business, including those in the emerging digital economy industries, needs to have more appropriate regulations whereby both corporations and humans fully consider climate change as well as the role they each need to play in addressing the cultural and social challenges.

Climate change is global. We live in a global economy and thanks to the internet we are creating a global village. Thus, our countries cannot keep acting in "the national interest," and corporations believing and acting only with the goal of "increasing profits" for the benefit of their shareholders.

The Sustainable Development Goals – attainable or fantastical?

The International Monetary Fund (IMF) is an organisation of 190 countries and works to achieve sustainable growth supporting economic policies that foster monetary cooperation and financial stability to increase productivity, job creation and economic well-being.[74]

Following the logic of the United Nations Sustainable Development Goals (SDGs)[75] – a set of 17 goals adopted by the United Nations in 2015 as a universal call to action to end poverty, protect the planet and ensure that by 2030 all people enjoy peace and prosperity – the IMF considers that "Development needs to be economically, socially and environmentally sustainable. The IMF helps

---

[74] International Monetary Fund (IMF), About the IMF: https://www.imf.org/en/About
[75] United Nations, Sustainable Development Goals: https://www.un.org/sustainabledevelopment/

countries around the world achieve the SDGs by working with them to develop the foundation for strong, sustainable economic growth, job creation and poverty reduction."[76]

The mantra of our global financial and economic system, however (followed by our institutions and our leaders), is the need for economic growth. And recently we just added sustainable. There is no politician in the world that perhaps would not mention it.

Our global village needs a green, circular economy whereby all resources are recovered and reused at their lifecycle's end. Thus, nothing is wasted.

The clear incompatibility lies with a global financial system that requires the system itself and corporations to grow. Achieving a circular sustainable global economy under our current economic understandings seems to be a delusion.

Indeed, we could consider the unlimited potential that applies to the concept of "money" and its creation, whereas our natural resources are not only limited but their savage exploitation and use has brought the devastation of climate change effects.

Perhaps we may not need economic growth, even if we think it is "sustainable". It has simply allowed the gap between rich and poor to widen.

The conundrum is that "No country has ever ended human deprivation without a growing economy and no country has ever ended ecological degradation with one." [77]

Maybe it is a conundrum because we as a species are constrained by our cultural and social common understandings. And perhaps such a conundrum would not exist if we effectively acknowledged and tackled the cultural and social challenges described above.

Furthermore, the fact is that the United Nations 17 SDGs are aspirations, not mandates. The tentative implication of this is reflected in the language we use more broadly about our current challenges, for instance when the WHO Chief said, when talking about COVID-19: "If we invest in health systems, we can bring this virus under control." It is safe to say the level of compliance required seems to be up in the air.

I guess our species still does not see tackling our current challenges,

---

[76] International Monetary Fund (IMF), The IMF and the Sustainable Development Goals: https://www.imf.org/en/Capacity-Development/what-we-do
[77] K Raworth op. cit. p 200

including climate change, as something essential that needs to be done, but rather as if we are talking as something nice to have, completely disregarding the potential extinction our species faces if we do not change.

Moreover, when we look at the likely level of compliance with the SDGs, it is not encouraging knowing that even fundamental international conventions such as ICESCR and CEDAW haven't been ratified by some fundamental actors in our global village. And even for those nations that have ratified ICESCR and CEDAW, their cultural acceptance and therefore level of progressive compliance has not been very effective, as the figures I outlined under Discrimination in the previous chapter show.

Even less encouraging is the fact that some lawyers around the world do not even know about ICESCR. Many of us think that when we talk about human rights, we are talking about our individual rights, expressed mainly in the International Covenant of Civil and Political Rights (ICCPR)[78], disregarding the clear interconnection that exists between both ICCPR and ICESCR as essential conventions to uphold human rights.

Not only human rights practitioners and advocates but collectively we could all be more aware of the paramount importance of the effective and progressive compliance with ICESCR in tackling our global challenges.

Adam Smith: a capitalist thinker and a moral philosopher

The Scottish economist Adam Smith is broadly considered the father of capitalism, but he was also a moral philosopher. Many know his An Inquiry into the Nature and Causes of the Wealth of Nations (commonly known as the Wealth of Nations), first published in 1776. However, not so many have got to read and appreciate the moral philosopher Smith in his first book, The Theory of Moral Sentiments. In this, he argues for a system of morality based on "sympathy," an idea more akin to modern-day empathy.[79]

It was long believed that the two books represented contradictory philosophies, with the first asking us to empathise with others to learn what's right and wrong, while the second focused on working in an individual's self-interest. However, today, scholars are aware of the

---

78 International Covenant on Civil and Political Rights (ICCPR)
79 https://www.adamsmithworks.org/documents/reading-guide-for-the-theory-of-moral-sentiments, Adam Smith Works, accessed 8 September 2022.

importance of viewing each book within the context of the other, and that such a viewing might help us get back to a more human-centred economics.

So, Mr Smith was both a capitalist thinker and a moral philosopher. And indeed, we can believe in capitalism and its benefits, and at the same time have moral values and act with integrity. In fact, I would argue you need both for the capitalist system to work.

But before looking more into Smith's fascinating theory of moral sentiments, acknowledging the historical cultural understandings at the time he lived is appropriate. For instance, the ideas of racial or class superiority were commonly accepted. These ideas were important, including for people from the Empire of Great Britain. Sadly, even today these ideas have seemingly persisted not only in the UK but in all the countries where descendants of people from UK live, including Australia, Canada, India and South Africa, just to name a few.

This anachronistic and obsolete idea of being superior was of course not only held by people from Great Britain but others too, including the Dutch, the Portuguese, and the Spanish "Conquistadores."

It may be argued many of us still unfortunately suffer from this type of superiority complex. Our tendencies to discriminate against others with our racist views, approaches and prejudice show our lack of knowledge, and evidence our ignorance. Many of us could therefore benefit by informing ourselves better, and perhaps even seeking professional help in this regard. After all, it is never too late to change.

It is also undeniable that Mr Smith, as for many people living in most continents around the world at that time, held patriarchal and deeply biased religious convictions. After all, at the time, slavery, dominance and the idea of being superior and the conquerors of "new lands" exploiting "inferior races" and "savages," were simply the norm – the common and accepted understandings.

If we could go back in time and bring Mr Smith to 2022, I think he would be screaming about how we haven't taken into consideration these two books not only in harmonious balance, but also how as a species we keep disregarding the current set of circumstances that makes our current understanding of capitalism simply unworkable.

Personally, thinking of the global challenges we have created, including our climate crisis, the Smith moral philosopher resonates with me more as we currently conceive our anthropocentric, individualistic understandings and approaches as "natural," whereas he clearly advocates for an ecocentric understanding and approach[80], the importance of equity and humanity, and the absurdity of approving cruelty and injustice, qualifying them as the most "dreadful stage of moral depravity."[81]

He knew that our purpose is to find "the happiness of mankind" and hence the importance of promoting the practice of truth, justice and humanity, and that the desire of humanity is not to be great but to be beloved. As he put it, "It is not in being rich that truth and justice would rejoice, but in being trusted and believed, recompences which those virtues must almost always acquire."[82]

Remember when we discussed Indigenous cultures and their legacies as something that we could learn from? Despite his historical cultural bias, even Smith seemed to somewhat acknowledge this:

"The savages in North America, we are told, assume upon all occasions the greatest indifference, and would think themselves degraded if they should ever appear in any respect to be overcome either by love, or grief, or resentment. Their magnanimity and self-command in this respect are almost beyond the conception of Europeans." [83]

Other important thoughts of Mr Smith include:

- "To restrain our selfish, and to indulge our benevolent, affections, constitutes the perfection of human nature… As to love our neighbour as we love ourselves is the great law of Christianity, so it is the great precept of nature to love ourselves only as we love our neighbour." [84]
- "All the members of human society stand in need of each other's assistance, and are likewise exposed to mutual injuries. Where the necessary assistance is reciprocally afforded from love, from gratitude, from friendship, and esteem, the society flourishes and is happy."[85]
- "society, however, cannot subsist among those who are at

---

[80] A Smith 'The Theory of Moral Sentiments' Part VII of Systems of Moral Philosophy (London: George Bell & Sons. York St, Covent Garden, and New York 1892) Digitised by Google. p 405
[81] Ibid pp 474, 475
[82] Ibid Part III of The Foundation of our Judgments Concerning our Own Sentiments and Conduct, and of the Sense of Duty, Chapter III – Of the Influence and Authority of Conscience. pp 235, 236
[83] Ibid Part V Of the Influence of Custom and Fashion Upon the Sentiments of Moral Approbation and Disapprobation, Chapter II – Of the Influence of Custom and Fashion Upon Moral Sentiments p 298
[84] Ibid Part I of the Propriety of Action, Chapter V – Of the Amiable and Respectable Virtues pp 27- 28
[85] Ibid Part II of Merit and Demerit, Chapter III – Of the Utility of this Constitution of Nature. p 124

all times ready to hurt and injure one another… society may subsist though not in the most comfortable state, without beneficence; but the prevalence of injustice must utterly destroy it."[86]

Adam Smith clearly understood that our individual self must never hurt or injure others to benefit ourselves[87], and that the principle of self-command is based on our sensibility to the feeling of others and what nowadays we may call empathy.[88]

His moral philosophy, despite its historical biases, still clearly has a lot to offer us – and it makes practical sense to understand his studies of morality precisely for the capitalist system to work.

The path to sustainable capitalism – Redistribution of income and wealth

The great depression in the 1930s, the Global Financial Crisis of 2007/2008, and the current social, political and economic crisis in so many countries worldwide throughout COVID-19 keeps showing us that the stability of the economic system is jeopardised when resources are concentrated in the hands of a few. By redistributing both income and wealth and tackling inequalities, we tackle the likelihood of economic recessions. The more equal a country is, the more likely the country is to experience stability and economic growth.[89]

Thus, to have a sustainable capitalism, we must tackle inequalities, and tackling inequalities requires us to change our discriminatory approaches and beliefs. Racism would need to cease, and so would gender inequality.

Having a sustainable capitalism requires us to have a shift in our mentality and consciousness. Our species needs to learn to stop creating enemies, conflict and war. We need to stop manufacturing, creating and developing weapons.

The business world cannot keep acting without social responsibility, supporting autocratic governments so that corporations can keep exploiting natural resources as they seem fit, disregarding Indigenous and minority groups while the ecological degradation of our planet continues.[90]

---

[86] Ibid. p 125
[87] Ibid Part III of The Foundation of our Judgments Concerning our Own Sentiments and Conduct, and of the Sense of Duty, Chapter III – Of the Influence and Authority of Conscience. p 195
[88] Ibid. pp 213, 214, 215
[89] K Raworth op. cit. pp 145,146,147, 148, 149,150, 151
[90] Ibid p 258

Sustainable capitalism = redistribution of both income and wealth = tackling inequalities = tackling discrimination (also tackling superiority complexes, gender inequality, racist prejudice and religious prejudice).

Taxation

Accepting that national interest is served by protecting multinationals[91] would need to change, and it seems the wheels might be somewhat in motion on this.

The Independent Commission for the Reform of International Corporate Taxation (ICRICT), for example, aims to promote the international corporate tax reform through a more inclusive discussion of international tax rules. The importance of ICRICT is perhaps not only due to its independence but the high level of expertise and diversity of its commissioners.[92]

Considering the findings of ICRICT thus far, it's clear that if we want to solve our global challenges, we also need a fairer global tax system – one that:

- Treats corporations as a unity, rather than considering corporations' subsidiaries and branches as separate entities entitled to separate treatment under tax law. Thus, tax avoidance through, for example, the 'double Irish with a Dutch sandwich' technique, or artificially creating loans through the subsidiaries whenever it is convenient to reduce profit, would no longer be possible.
- Sets a minimum corporate tax rate, so that the race to the bottom in corporate taxation is avoided.
- Provides rules that are fairer, clearer, easier to administer to reduce the scope of conflict.
- Has a governance understanding that states its obligations to comply with human rights, hence a universal international tax that considers the diverse needs and capacities of all countries.

Despite the good deeds of the ICRICT, it is perhaps only when we

---

[91] Independent Commission for the Reform of International Corporate Taxation 'The OECD has not delivered. The world needs and answer now, not further delays' https://www.icrict.com/press-release/2020/10/11/52n5njz8ja42ukkws0z7vgppuuse4b

[92] Independent Commission for the Reform of International Corporate Taxation 'International Corporate Tax reform: Towards a fair and comprehensive solution' (October 2019) https://static1.squarespace.com/static/5a0c602bf43b5594845abb81/t/5d979e6dc5f7cb7b66842c49/15 70217588721/ICRICT-INTERNATIONAL+CORPORATE+TAX+REFORM.pdf

as a species have tackled our cultural and social challenges that we may be able to see that corporations no longer hire legal and accounting firms to look for loopholes to avoid paying taxes or defend "their" interest in courts worldwide.

Maybe only then, when corporations behave and act with clear social responsibility, would we be able to end subsidies and tax exceptions to corporations. Tax havens will cease to exist, because we have eventually realised how nonsensical, inhumane and unsustainable they were.

Billionaires – The power to tackle climate change

It is clear we need to change our current cultural, social and economic understandings. We all need to buy in.

Thinking still in binary terms, some of us look at our business leaders and entrepreneurs as a source of inspiration, with admiration and respect for their knowledge, innovation, creativity and discipline. Others may feel disappointed with some leaders' lack of social responsibility, with their depiction not dissimilar to Charles Montgomery Burns.

But it is simply biased to see businesspeople through these common binary lenses.

I think many businesspeople worldwide understand not only that the current financial and economic system is unsustainable, but also that the wealth they have created or inherited is also at stake if they or we don't properly tackle the causes of climate change.

I see that billionaires certainly have the power to save our species and tackle climate change.

Billionaires could inspire all of us to start doing the right thing. They could lead by example.

Many billionaires donate money to reduce their taxes, and many also embrace the happiness and positivity philanthropy brings. However, as our current global challenges keep showing, this is not enough.

If we want to keep our current global and financial economic system going, we need to make some adjustments. It must be sustainable for real. It must be inclusive. The importance of substantial gender equality in tackling our challenges, as mentioned earlier, is paramount.

I believe women could change the course of our history, and our current path of self-destruction.

Indeed, it not only brings pride but plenty of hope to see, among many others, Greta Thunberg, Alexandria Ocasio-Cortez, Jacinda Ardern and Kamala Harris leading the way for change.

Call me loco or a dreamer but I imagine women like Melinda French Gates, Francoise Bettencourt Meyers, Alice Walton, Mackenzie Scott, Julia Koch, Yang Huiyan, Wu Yajun, Zhong Huijuan, Jacqueline Mars, Susane Klatten, or Laurene Powell Jobs, to name just a few, in the same room (virtually) discussing how to tackle climate change. They probably (hopefully) already are.

Imagine there is among them already a clear understanding of the importance not only of substantial gender equality, but of redistribution of wealth and of having a more egalitarian global village in order to tackle our climate crisis.

Imagine, businesswomen not waiting for governments to save us (because they know they won't), instead they come up with a common agreement whereby:

- Their corporations are treated as a unit for tax purposes.
- They accept 25% tax as the minimum rate. (There's no race to the bottom but to the top. Who may be the billionaires that agree to the highest tax, in order to lead the change for our species survival?)
- They, their family members, and their companies' executives take the money out of tax havens and pay the agreed taxes.
- 25% of their profits are transferred to an international fund dedicated exclusively to tackling climate change (creating renewable means of energy, adaptation, mitigation, and disaster relief – in the poorest regions of our planet and where capital and help is most needed).
- They implement public, transparent monitoring and reporting mechanisms of the international trust fund's activities and developments.

Now imagine, given our species' sense of competitiveness, how male billionaires may feel about the "radical" agreement reached by women billionaires. Particularly, when men (us) are the ones who have brought about the climate crisis.

Probably I am indeed too loco, but I could see people like Bill Gates, Warren Buffett, Jeff Bezos, Bernard Arnault, Elon Musk, Mark

Zuckerberg, Larry Page, Larry Ellison, Mukesh Amabani and Sergey Brin, among many others adopting the agreement.

They all could inspire not only other billionaires worldwide, but also millionaires, well-off people, and everyone around the world to start doing not only what is right but what needs to be done.

The alternative is, don't do anything, let's see what happens, wait until the economic and social system collapses.

Eventually, they'd have 'billions of dollars' that have no value, and more importantly, know that their children and future descendants would not enjoy the wealth they created, because there will be no liveable planet for them.

And in no way am I trying to point fingers at these particular billionaires. The names are used only for illustrative purposes. There are over two thousand billionaires on our planet,[93] some of whom may just need to lead the way out of the climate crisis.

Reflecting again on the agreement I've imagined – perhaps dreamed – those women creating and agreeing to, I know the figures I outline are a lot of money. 50% of their businesses' profits, in fact. But if everyone buys in, nobody loses anything. We all win. Our species may have more chances not only of survival but of living in a sustainable, more humane and dignified global village moving forward.

Billionaires could save us from the challenges our species created.

Billionaires could indeed be the saviours of our species in the pages of human history.

From a practical point of view, what is more important anyway? To increase the amount of one's wealth by some more billions, be in the top 10–100–1,000 billionaires on the Forbes list, or making sure there is a liveable planet for our descendants, and to have humanity's respect, admiration and pride in the billionaire's legacy saving our species from social and ecological collapse?

---

[93] Forbes, The real-time billionaires list: https://www.forbes.com/real-time-billionaires/#267e8bdc3d78

6

CIVIL SOCIETY AND THE GUIDING PRINCIPLES ON BUSINESS AND HUMAN RIGHTS

There is currently no international convention regarding business and human rights, although we do have The Guiding Principles on Business and Human Rights[94] developed by Professor John Gerard Ruggie under the direction of the United Nations. However, even though these could form a good framework for businesses to make sure they respect and comply with fundamental human rights, they are an example of soft law – that is, a legal instrument that does not have the capacity to be enforced. In other words, it is not a binding document.

Although it would of course be ideal to have a binding treaty regarding business and human rights, it does not look promising in the current geopolitical climate. In the meantime, we have some options.

International law obligations including human rights are generally considered to be state-based, and thus for the business world and in particular large corporations, any attempts to create an international treaty regulating non-state actors and imposing obligations on corporations and business enterprises is seen as the privatisation of human rights.[95]

This perspective is perhaps validly disputed, however, with the

---

[94]https://www.ohchr.org/sites/default/files/Documents/Publications/GuidingPrinciplesBusinessHR EN.pdf, accessed 8 September 2022.
[95] J Ruggie 'Just Business Multinational Corporations and Human Rights' (W.W Norton & Company Ltd 2013) Introduction, [xvii].

Universal Declaration of Human Rights. Even though it is not a treaty, this declaration, with its 30 articles, is considered customary international law. Regarding business in particular, articles 29 and 30 – with their references to everyone's duty in a democratic society and the fact that nothing in the Declaration could be interpreted as implying that any State, group or person has any right to engage in activity or acts aimed at destroying any of the rights and freedoms within it – seemed to open the doors to include non-state actors such as corporations.[96]

Indeed, The Universal Declaration is widely accepted together with both the International Covenant on Civil and Political Rights (ICCPR) and the International Covenant on Economic, Social and Cultural Rights (ICESCR), as the International Bill of Rights.

According to Professor Ruggie, the field of business and human rights should also include consideration of the International Labour Organisation's Declaration on Fundamental Principles and Rights at Work.[97]

Despite the ongoing controversy between the supporters of large corporations and those who believe in the importance of the application of human rights standards to corporate behaviour, it is undeniable that the practical relationship between business and human rights, and thus the guiding principles, provides a framework for businesses to make sure they respect and comply with fundamental human rights.

And despite the criticism of the guiding principles by some scholars, academics and activists, in particular because of the guiding principles' aspirational and non-binding characteristics, it is fair to say that given the nature and characteristics of the mandate given to Ruggie by the UN, as well as the foreseeable repercussions for the business world (even as a soft law instrument), it was certainly a very complex environment to accommodate and meet the expectations by all interested parties.

Credit to Ruggie, he raised funds, conducted research through law firms on a pro bono basis, and Civil Society organisations were participants in the consultations. As he has acknowledged,

---

[96] D Weissbrodt and M Krugger 'Human Rights Responsibilities of Business as Non-State Actors', in P Alston (Non- State Actors and Human Rights) 330,331.
[97] United Nations 'Guiding Principles on Business and Human Rights' The Corporate Responsibility to Respect Human Rights 12 https://www.ohchr.org/Documents/Publications/GuidingPrinciples BusinessHR_EN.pdf

organisations such as Global Witness and Oxfam also worked closely with him.[98]

To see the role of civil society in the UN guiding principles, is important to keep in mind the global crisis of effective public governance, and the growing demand of corporate social responsibility.

The guiding principles as described by Ruggie should read as a trilogy, namely: protecting, respecting and providing a remedy framework, thus respective obligations derive from the States to protect, businesses to respect and those who are harmed to be provided with remedies.

At a glance, it may look like there is not a particular and defined role assigned to civil society, however, the guiding principles constitute transparent standards that not only CEOs of corporations or business at large should implement or consider, but more importantly members of civil society such as unions, investors, universities, NGOs, public servants, human rights activists, and we as consumers, can hold both ourselves and corporations accountable to.

Indeed, it's easier for us as consumers to simply say that business should comply with those and there is no actual role for us or that nothing should be demanded of us.

On the contrary, we are the ones using their services and buying their products, many are shareholders of those corporations, and constitute one of their main assets as employees.

Back now to the idea of a binding treaty regarding business and human rights – this does not look like a promising proposition right now. We must consider the reality of the duration of the negotiations involved in developing such a treaty (business and human rights treaty attempts started in the 1970s), in addition to the fact that, as Ruggie notes, treaties require certain degrees of abstraction or generality to leave margin for states to implement in their jurisdictions. [99]

Thus, how many states where most large corporations come from or operate in are likely to ratify such a treaty? How long would it take to introduce that treaty in jurisdictions where domestic legislation is required? And what degree of actual compliance would the eventual treaty have?

---

[98] J Ruggie op. cit. Introduction, [xiii].
[99] Ibid, p 13.

These are certainly not easy questions to answer. I'm not saying that these well-known difficulties should be a deterrent to continue working towards a treaty. Perhaps though, we could focus our efforts for now on looking towards creating separate, transnational, legally binding international agreements where corporations, depending on the sector and industry, are an integral part of the agreements. After all, without a binding mechanism, the likelihood that damages would be compensated by the judiciary or that corporations would voluntarily establish alternative mechanisms to provide remedy when damage occurs, appears to be highly unlikely.

Despite the clear differences between hard and soft law, the guiding principles as an expression of the latter could be proven more effective if the members of civil society, including universities, NGOs working in the field of human rights and development, and people at large, put more pressure on governments so that at regional and state levels legislation is introduced and policy is developed following the three pillars of the guiding principles.

Their compliance must be duly enforced, and when there are damages caused by business, the need for an independent judiciary or alternative mechanisms of justice must be provided to make sure that proper compensation is afforded.

The guiding principles hence provide a benchmark that can be seen as a clear expectation for civil society to be proactive and engage, not only to take accountability as consumers and investors but also to be empowered to bring accountability to both governments and businesses. In this respect, Ruggie says, the potential power of the guiding principles is not in their legal enforceability but rather their moral and political authority.

Without denying the importance of having binding legislation or binding agreements to access the courts or alternative mechanism of dispute resolution, the real success of any norm is neither its incorporation in international treaties nor its adoption in constitutions or domestic legislation by States. Real success comes from persons both natural and legal understanding its content, purpose and the nature of the obligations, as well as cultural acceptance and respectful obedience of it.

Thus, as happens perhaps with most human rights norms and

customary international law, higher levels of compliance are seen when more resources and a diversity of channels are used to inform and educate the members of society.

Education on the guiding principles is therefore without a doubt one avenue to guarantee a culture of business and human rights where appropriate corporate social responsibility is the culturally accepted norm.

In this endeavour, the role of civil society is paramount to fulfilling its role in the business and human rights agenda.

In this respect, a civil society that shares fundamental values of peace, ecological awareness and respect for the environment and the principles of environmental law – finding a balance between the liberal, anthropocentric view of the world with a much-needed ecocentric understanding and approach, as well as respect for human rights – is key as an effective actor of change.[100]

Civil society at large represented by the people's power, rather than corporations' instrumental, structural and discursive power, has a difficult but determinant role to play in making sure we take accountability for our own actions. It also has a role in making sure there is enough pressure on both governments and corporations to get the guiding principles broadly implemented, such that corporations' adoption of fundamental human rights happens not only as part of their policies and codes of conduct, but also their business objectives and core values.[101]

---

[100] P Alston "The 'Not-A-Cat' Syndrome: Can the International Human Rights Regime Accommodate Non-State Actors?" (Non-State Actors and Human Rights 2005) 22.

[101] J Ruggie "The Multinational as a Global Institution: Power, Authority and Relative Autonomy" (Regulation and Governance 2017) 5-9; The Economist Intelligence Unit' The Road from Principles to Practice: Today's challenges for Business in Respecting Human Rights (2015) 22.

7
ARE WE READY?

While watching one of the Harry Potter movies back in 2019 with my then six-year-old daughter Sophie, we saw the scene where Harry realises he is holding the Elder Wand. Ron asks, "What are we going to do with it? That's the most powerful wand in the world. With that we'd be invincible." I paused the movie and asked Sophie what Harry should do. With the wisdom that most kids naturally have and that we only hope our leaders have, Sophie quickly replied, "Destroy it." When I asked her why, she responded firmly and quickly, "So that no baddie could ever use it again."

When we have so many leaders around the world still telling us that for the "peace and security" of "our nation" we need to keep investing billions of dollars in the military, including weapons (even nuclear), it's time we wake up. Our species will not be more secure by continuing to invest in military means. Some of our most brilliant minds, from Carl Sagan to Stephen Hawkins, tell us about the risk of our military technological advances, and that the paramount need to demilitarise the world economy and achieve substantial achieve gender equality is crystal clear.

As a human rights advocate and lawyer who was born, raised and lived in a country of conflict for 26 years, and has been lucky to travel and experience different cultures around the world, I understand and know firsthand that military, physical means do not solve conflicts and do not bring peace and security. I'd like to think that our species is hopefully starting to understand that demilitarisation of the world economy is a must.

I believe we are ready to tackle the global challenges we have created, including climate change. We are more conscious human rights advocates.

We all are learning to not just tolerate but embrace and celebrate the beauty and benefits diversity brings to our global village. To learn to question ourselves, change our common cultural understandings and stop our discriminatory approaches, attitudes and beliefs, is the test our species has.

The word "love" in this book is repeated 28 times. Learning to respect and love others even when they look, sound or appear different from us, would set humankind free.

I wish there was a magic pill to make us more respectful of the inherent dignity of every human being on this planet. If we have learned to dominate, to believe we are superior, to discriminate, to be racist and non-tolerant, we could also learn a different way.

Despite the negative effects of the COVID-19 pandemic and the still-growing number of casualties, it could also mean a historical turning point for our species. Perhaps 2020 and the years immediately after it would make us individually and collectively understand our global challenges better. We might then be able to change our current cultural, social and economic understandings, so we can effectively adapt and guarantee our species' survival.

We could be a species finding equilibrium and adapting to the effects of climate change with a conscious, non-discriminatory approach and beliefs, with substantial gender equality, in a non-militarised world and a sustainable green, circular economy, with renewable means of energy as a fundamental part of our socio-economic and political system.

Due to the ongoing global health and poverty issues, and the already existing crisis of refugees and stateless people, we eventually may come to understand the paramount importance of respecting and complying not only with the International Covenant on Civil and Political Rights (ICCPR) but the equally important International Covenant on Economic, Social and Cultural Rights (ICESCR).

The compliance of the above two main international human rights conventions, however, should not be left to the sovereignty of States or the generosity and free will of citizens. It must come from design. A global design for our global village.

I understand many people may feel uneasy, doubtful or perhaps think that it is naïve to think we could change our current cultural, socio-economic and political understandings. I honestly think that on the contrary, it is naïve to continue the current path of self-destruction. If we keep following the same cultural and socio-economic understandings, the result would be the extinction of our species.

As Adam Smith said, "Justice… is the main pillar that upholds the whole edifice. If it is removed, the great, the immense fabric of human society, must in a moment crumble into atoms."[102]

A just, fair, prosperous and sustainable world is a dream. I could not agree more.

It is a dream that if we all collectively believe in, could become our reality.

---

[102] A Smith 'The Theory of Moral Sentiments' Part II of Merit and Demerit, Chapter III – Of the Utility of this Constitution of Nature (London: George Bell & Sons. York St, Covent Garden, and New York 1892) Digitised by Google. P. 125

8
UNITED BY A GLOBAL IDENTITY

We can properly address our global challenges and reduce the devastating effects of climate change, and in doing so, tackle discrimination. We can tackle the cultural, social and economic challenges we are facing head on.

There is no need to keep insisting, with our binary lenses, on winners and losers. We could all win. We could develop more empathy and compassion for those who have been historically discriminated against, as well as those who are already in the process of losing not only their land, but with their land, their sense of culture and identity.[103]

Creating a safer, fairer, more just and more inclusive global village for us as a species should not be a lofty goal but rather our common understanding of who we are.

This is something that we can achieve. It would bring pride, not as individuals that are part of one country, nation, or region of the world, but as citizens of planet Earth.

We can dare to imagine a new economic and socio-political system where there is not only a future, but one where everyone has similar opportunities to live an honest, dignified and sustainable life.

There is always hope. Our ability to create, innovate, set goals, achieve and explore is undeniably at the core of what makes us humans.

We invented weapons to exert dominance. We also invented

---

[103] S Kirsch 'Engaged Anthropology, Politics Beyond the Text' (University of California Press 2018) 161, 162, 163, 164

religions, countries, nations, flags, currencies, political, social and economic systems, corporations, and the financial system. We also created human rights.

All those inventions are just that, inventions. We cannot keep arguing that economic growth, increasing profits and continuing to accumulate material possessions is what we need, what we want or what would make us prosperous.

We are at a point in history where, if we want to survive, we need to dare to explore a different system, a different reality – one in which the different ecosystems and the environment are a priority; where racism is truly not tolerated; where success, and the achievement of targets and goals, are measured by the level of prosperity we all enjoy as a result.

Within this though, the term 'prosperity' needs to be redefined. Prosperity can no longer be attached to the simplistic capitalist view that what matters most is how much money we have in our bank accounts, how many properties we have in our portfolios, or how much we can spend on luxury goods.

Prosperity could have a different meaning – one that also is not a goal but rather a reality we all shape, where every human being has access to water, food, employment, shelter, health, education and recreation.

This is not ground-breaking. It is what we figured out after the devastation of the first and second world wars when most nations around the world adopted the International Covenant on Economic, Social and Cultural Rights (ICESCR), even though we have not yet had success in fully adopting and progressively complying with it.

It is not about getting back to the old and unworkable model of socialist societies either, as explained in the social challenge Neither Capitalism nor Socialism in an earlier chapter.

Prosperity may be better understood when we give different ideas, theories and concepts the possibility to interact and be applied – the universal basic salary, a green economy and a circular economy could be applied and introduced to our consciousness and into our everyday lives.

If we manage to survive the global challenges, a shift in our common understandings would occur.

We will perhaps evolve, creating a reality whereby even concepts such as discrimination, racism, refugees, economic competitiveness, business advantage, powerful vs powerless, cheap vs expensive, cost vs benefit, rich vs poor, educated vs uneducated, right-wing vs left-wing, and even human rights, cease to exist – relegated, perhaps, to the history books.

We could create a new system that is in tune with the natural world, where we depart decisively from the dominance, exertion of power, prejudice, racism and double standards that characterise our current capitalist system, enhanced by our social and political structures.

Some could say that this is simple wishful thinking, without any possibility to become reality.

I say yes, that would be the case if we won't question our beliefs.

Perhaps a simple retort to this resistance is the fact that Norway is already integrating the concept of the universal basic salary. Other countries and regions, including Alaska, North Carolina, India and Kenya, are also trying it.

Moreover, business leaders including Jack Ma, Mark Zuckerberg and Elon Musk see that unemployment will continue to rise due to automation and developments in artificial intelligence, and that would likely require the adoption of the universal basic salary in the future anyway.

Furthermore, it is in our DNA to innovate, create, change and evolve. Some may consider Elon Musk and Jeff Bezos crazy for thinking our species could potentially be living on other planets in the future. I don't. Instead, I believe the cruellest representation of insanity is what we are currently experiencing. We all keep believing in a system that at its core is no longer viable and is utterly broken. The sooner we understand, acknowledge and start working towards a different system, the better the chances of our survival.

When we redefine what we now understand as our political, economic and social system, and decide to put in place a different one that hopefully considers the above reflections, the effects will likely be seen by:

- The creativity, innovation, and prosperity of our species – understood not just as well-being standards but a sense of fulfillment and an identity that is not only shaped by being proud of belonging to the human species, but one that found richness and purpose in finding equilibrium.
- Finding not only balance with nature in a sustainable world, but within our families, in our inner worlds, and in the

different areas of knowledge of human and non-human experience that every individual decides to explore and contribute to this planet.

If we manage to create such a reality, the level of growth we will achieve in the arts, sciences, technology, and the different fields of knowledge that we would discover as we evolve would be exponential.

Perhaps when we are in that reality, only then, may we be ready to head to the stars.

9
MY JOURNEY

I was born and raised in Colombia, South America. I studied law there in the early 90s and practiced as a lawyer for several years. My legal formation is therefore based in a civil law system.

Despite the undeniable history of conflict and violation of human rights in Colombia, in 1991, we changed our aging Constitution and elevated human rights to the category of constitutional rights, so my academic and legal formation was based on human rights too.

From this context of human rights within a civil law tradition, I moved to Australia in 2001, where a range of personal, work (professional and non-professional roles), business and academic experiences enabled me to develop a strong understanding of the common law system too.

This book has been in the making for the last 6 years, but it is not just the product of those years.

It is the product of having been born, raised and lived in Colombia for 26 years, studying a law degree and a postgraduate degree and then working as a commercial lawyer there. Of migrating to Australia in my mid-20s and being born again in a sense, learning English as a second language (20 years in the making now), living on a different continent, sharing and learning from diverse cultures, and learning from diverse work and business experiences as well as vocational and academic experiences. Of being fortunate enough to be supported by the Australian government to study a Master of Human Rights in what is generally considered one of the top Australian universities, Melbourne

University. Of being, from an early age, attracted to international affairs. Of being a traveller, always curious, reading about the cultures, history and trying to learn at least some words of the languages of my next destinations, so I could see, experience, learn and connect with the locals and enjoy the journeys more deeply. Of extending my family not only to Colombian and Venezuelan ties but also counting Argentinian Italian Australians, Polish Australians, Samoan Australians, Czechs, and Australians descended from the UK as part of it.

Growing up, I was what a psychologist might now call a highly sensitive child. For the parents out there with highly sensitive kids, for teachers, employers and the general community – there is nothing wrong with us.

We are highly observant, perceptive and responsive to art and music. We tend not to enjoy crowded places, or loud environments, or loud people (being from South America though, I had to get used to both. Indeed, by Aussie standards, I may be considered a loud person). We have been described as having difficulties going with the flow – we experience everything in life perhaps a hundred times more intensely than "the average" person. Some of our more positive characteristics are our creativity and deep empathy for others.[104] That's also perhaps why I wrote this book.

Speaking of empathy, now more than ever, being able to feel empathy and compassion towards our fellow human beings is deeply needed to properly address our global challenges.

The way that highly sensitive people may perhaps feel about others is encapsulated in the words of Walt Whitman when he wrote, "I do not ask the wounded person how he feels, I myself become the wounded person."[105]

In sharing this with you, I hope we continue questioning our general tendency to look for labels, to put people in certain moulds so "they" make sense to "us" according to "our" culture, religions and beliefs. Although it's generally accepted to refer to some people as people with disabilities, for example, I simply do not accept the term. In general, I believe people have diverse levels of ability.

I remember Zane McKenzie, a fantastic trainer in Melbourne,

---

[104] S Rodman 'How to talk to your kids about your divorce' (Adams Media 2015) p. 65,66
[105] Ibid p. 89; W Whitman 'Song of Myself' (1892 version)
https://www.poetryfoundation.org/poems/45477/song-of-myself-1892-version

Australia. He has cerebral palsy and was doing a session on how to engage with people with different levels of ability. Zane mentioned that one day he was in the foyer of a building and approached the reception to ask where the toilets were. The receptionist started to reply with "The disabled toilets are located…," when Zane interrupted her and said, "I don't need a disabled toilet; I need one that works!"

People with different abilities as well as people that may be experiencing disadvantage are still taboo in many societies worldwide. Given the challenges of climate change and those the ongoing COVID-19 pandemic has brought in terms of exacerbating domestic violence and creating more mental health problems, there is a need for better education to address these taboos.

Unfortunately, it is still common to read articles and books of psychologists and mental health practitioners referring to people "who are mentally ill." I would take this opportunity to set the record straight. There are no people mentally ill, there are people experiencing mental health problems or challenges. They may recover or they may not, but stating the condition in present tense as if it is a permanent state, is simply incorrect.

Furthermore, most of us have experienced situations in our lives in which our mental health was impacted or have someone in our family who has experienced such challenges, whether they were related to alcohol or drug addiction, anxiety, depression, losing someone close, or navigating a divorce, to name just a few. There is no shame in admitting it.

Like many migrants in Australia, I have experienced discrimination. Being from South America, you are used to simply toughening up, knowing that the world is a difficult place and that you must keep moving forward.

However, when it has happened in diverse circumstances and when you feel that even some close to you don't understand or acknowledge what you have experienced, it brings a different level of complexity to your life journey. To be fair, it's difficult for some to really understand discrimination properly when they may never have experienced it nor felt they have suffered it.

In sharing this with you, I neither accept the adoption of a "poor me" mentality nor believe myself a victim. Indeed, knowing and seeing the level of discrimination for instance people from African, Asian and Indigenous ancestry (to name some) must deal with, it has always made me feel the need to toughen up, to be stronger.

I share the belief perhaps of most people who migrate to other countries, if you let yourself down because you believe you have suffered discrimination, or adopt a victim mentality, you lose – you allow yourself to become a second-class citizen.

Through my human rights studies and developing a better understanding of what the scientific community has been unanimously saying for decades about the effects of climate change, I could no longer be in the comfortable position of ignoring or dismissing the effects of climate change. However, like many worldwide, I withdrew for a while.

In full lockdown in Melbourne throughout 2020 due to COVID-19, I relied on my instinctive, resilient nature. I shook and picked myself up, and this book started to take shape.

At the end of 2020, we moved to Brisbane, in the sunshine state of Queensland, Australia, and I began rebuilding my personal and professional life.

Regardless of how seemingly severe or not a particular condition or disadvantage may appear, every human being is unique and has unique skills and talents that could be used to benefit themselves, their families and communities in general.

As a global community, we can develop better understandings and untap the potential that people with different levels of ability have to offer to our global village.

Let me for a moment also briefly tell you about the ones who are to blame for me writing this book. My parents. They are both educators.

Mum is from the small village of San Joaquin in the Department of Santander in Colombia, South America. Many Germans migrated to Santander and other regions of Colombia from the 16th century, so my grandfather, like many Colombians, had German ancestors. My grandmother passed away in a car accident when Mum was a child, but judging by family photos, grandma was clearly a Guane Indigenous woman.

Mum has fair skin and blue eyes. She is small but extraordinarily big in spirit and generosity. Daily, I witnessed her ability to listen, to care and to not judge people, at home and at the Colegio Nacional de San Simón in the city of Ibagué, Colombia – a public high school where she worked for most of her career, and the school my dad, my two brothers and I also graduated from.

Many years ago, I went to surprise Mum at the school, and I noticed some of her students were calling her "Mami." Throughout the years I got used to hearing students calling her Mum, and people stopping her quite often on the streets of Ibagué to introduce their own kids to her.

Looking back, it's a nice feeling to know the level of connection, respect and love many generations of Ibaguereños feel towards Mum. She was a biology and chemistry teacher, then an academic coordinator. She retired as the principal of another public school.

Dad is from a small town called Chaparral in the department of Tolima. Dad's ancestors are Spaniards and I hope the Pijao, the Indigenous population of Tolima, also run in my veins.

Dad is an agronomical engineer. He was also a professor at different universities and worked as a real estate and tax valuer of rural and urban properties for the government and in the private sector. Dad also helped coffee growers in the North of Tolima to set up their first cooperative in the region and provided technical assistance to agricultores (farmers) in the north of Tolima.

During school holidays, my two brothers and I took turns to be with Dad while he was providing technical assistance to farmers.

The routine was to wake up at 4am, go to the marketplace, have a tinto (black coffee) and a desayuno (breakfast) while talking to the locals, then go visiting the farms, walking through crops, meeting farmers, and coming back at the end of the day to have a shower, dinner and go to sleep. And then do it all again the next day.

Some of the farmers were very poor so I did wonder how they were able to pay for Dad's services, but Dad always wanted to help. Both Mum and Dad taught my two brothers and I the importance of sharing.

I grew up seeing Dad coming back to Ibague carrying different types of tropical fruits, nuts, cheese, meats, fish, chicken and rice that were given to him by his clients and friends.

When my younger brother was diagnosed with bronchitis when he was little, I urged my parents to research (at the time the mighty Google wasn't around), and we found that replacing cow's milk for goat milk may be helpful. Not long after, Dad arrived one day at our flat on the second floor with a goat given to him by one of his mates.

So yes, we had a goat living in the apartment with us for a little while. And yes, I would agree that the idea of a goat living in a flat in Colombia may sound like it's straight out of one of the stories of Gabriel García Marquéz, but it happened.

These were life lessons not only of what parents do for their children, but of cooperation, solidarity and sharing as essential forces of society. When I look back, it was also my first appreciation of seeing money not as a currency but for what money really is, an exchange of values.

Money is indeed an exchange of values. If you haven't watched the economist-banker Tony Greenham in his Ted Talk on money as a relationship, it is worth checking out. Tony mentions how most money is created by private banks, with banking being a system driven by short-term profit, it is inherently unstable. He reminds us how in Mesopotamia, money was created without debt, without interest, without inflation and without banking crashes.

According to Tony, "Money is not metal, it's trust. Money is a social relationship. We must not let money control us. As long as we have creativity and trust in our communities, we can never ever run out of money."[106]

Both of my parents are still alive and living in Ibagué, Colombia. They survived the COVID-19 pandemic (as of July 2022, Colombia has had over 140,000 deaths due to it). I could not be prouder of them. This book is also a way to honour their love and teachings, as well as Colombians.

As for me, well, like many in the American continent (the descendants of Africans, Indigenous and Europeans) I'm mestizo – a mix of European and Indigenous blood. My personal history is influenced by the history of my native Colombia. The history of Colombia is the history of humanity, it is a history of conflict. Colombia has been in conflict since Europeans went there more than 500 years ago.

We "kicked out" the Spaniards in 1810 then had our civil war from 1860 to 1862. This was followed, from 1899 to 1902, by a conflict known as La Guerra de los mil días (the 1000-day war) between the two political parties of Liberal and Conservador. By then, a new oligarchy had taken possession of Colombia.

---

[106] T Greenham 'Money is a social relationship.' TEDx Leiden, 29 November 2012, available at https://www.youtube.com/watch?v=f1pS1emZP6A

The entrenched social and economic inequalities in Colombia brought the creation of different guerrilla movements throughout the 60s, 70s, 80s and 90s. Instead of bringing more inclusiveness and a more socially, politically, and economically egalitarian society, we insisted on fighting fire with fire.

There's been different peace processes, in particular one in 1990–1991 that brought the demobilisation of various guerrilla groups and the creation of The Constituent Assembly of Colombia that modified the ageing 1886 Constitution. Thus, a more contemporary Colombian Constitution was born in 1991.

In 1995, our answer to the guerrilla groups, given the Colombian Army seemed insufficient, was the creation of Convivir – citizen security groups and networks of informants, supported by the political and legal system.

The medicine resulted more costly than the illness. The Convivir became paramilitary groups, who have also committed many atrocities in Colombia.

I have lost the count of the killings and massacres of innocent fellow Colombians by the different parties to the conflict. And I have seen first-hand how the social fabric of society is affected.

I studied at a public high school where some of my classmates came to class having just had aguapanela (hardened sugar cane juice with water) for breakfast, while also going to school with a classmate who, due to the risk of her being kidnapped, had to often be accompanied by bodyguards.

These experiences made me realise at a young age the importance of an egalitarian society, including good public education for all. Scandinavian countries seemingly understand this, after all you think twice about doing something negative when "the others" are your mates from school.

They also opened the doors for a better understanding of what non-discrimination, compassion, tolerance and kindness may be.

There were so many people with nothing to lose, so stealing, kidnapping and acts of terrorism occurred, and in some regions, unfortunately continue to occur.

Living in Colombia meant that as I saw that not even the "privileged" and wealthy could really enjoy "their" money. I wasn't one of these wealthy individuals, and neither are my parents. I could describe myself in economic terms as an average Joe – and perhaps, despite the ups and downs of life, a happy average Joe.

While living in Colombia, even though I was in good health, with a stable and well-paid job working for a trustee company that was a subsidiary of one of the main banks in Colombia, and with strong social and family relationships, I felt I needed a change.

I found it difficult to tolerate not only the killings of people, many of them defenders of human rights and Indigenous people, but also seeing how the deaths of ordinary Colombians reported regularly on the news were starting to desensitize most of us (a clear self-defence mechanism).

When I say deaths of ordinary Colombians, I refer to both those killed through being caught in the conflict, and the poorest in society who did not have access to education and to choose what to do in life. For too many Colombians, it was joining either the Colombian army, the guerrilla, the paramilitary or the drug cartels. In many cases, they didn't even decide this for themselves.

It was breaking me to see the level of poverty, Internally Displaced People (IDP), people experiencing homelessness, and kids on the streets selling candies and cigarettes instead of being at school or playing and enjoying life.

I studied law in the early 90s in Bogotá at the Universidad Externado de Colombia, when Pablo Escobar was head of the Cartel de Medellin and "Los Extraditables" were in war against the Colombian government (from 1984 to 1993). So, we all lived through bombs and acts of terrorism.

I know it may sound strange, but somehow, as millions of others around the world who have been in regions of conflict do, we just got used to that, and pretty much just got on with our lives.

To be fair, not always but historically, most of the Colombian conflict has taken place in the forest, in rural areas and small towns. Perhaps that's why there are Colombians that continue to support the idea that peace is achievable by "destroying the enemy" and through military means – because they've never really seen it.

In Colombia, as perhaps happens in many places worldwide, it is not about knowing that military means will never bring peace. Rather, it is about continuing a narrative that keeps the usual suspects in power and the businesses of weapons, security and war going.

In the roller coaster of life, not everything is within the binary of bad or good.

After many years of terrorism, we had Antanas Mockus, the son of Lithuanian immigrants (his father an engineer, his mum an artist), a Colombian mathematician and philosopher who quit his job as chancellor of the National University of Colombia in 1993 and ran for mayor of Bogotá D.C.

Antanas is a visionary, loved by most Colombians. He brought cultura ciudadana, 'citizenship culture,' into the political agenda and reminded us of the importance of moral norms that honour and respect human life, gender equality, ethical values, a more egalitarian society, and a balanced life.

Mockus was mayor of Bogotá from 1995 to 1997, then 2001 to 2003. He brought social awareness using pedagogy and humour as a way of transforming social behaviour and solving problems. Some of his contributions included a "Night without Men", where the city's men were asked to stay home and look after the children while women went out. There were free open-air concerts, and the Ciclovía, a concept still admired and emulated worldwide, where during certain days and hours of the week, only bicycles and no other vehicles are allowed on some of the busiest city roads.

I think of the number of tons of GHG emissions Colombians have avoided by putting such a simple measure in place, and the positive effects on the population's well-being due to the possibility of exercising outdoors while breathing fresh air without the pollution of millions of cars.

Indeed, the creativity and civic culture embodied by Antanas has helped many cities: 56 cities in Colombia, 12 cities in Latin America, including in Mexico, Dominican Republic, Panama, Venezuela, Ecuador, Bolivia, Brazil, Paraguay, Uruguay, and in Europe, Stockholm in Sweden.[107]

Imagine if every city in the world had one day of the week where cars, buses and trucks are not allowed and people could enjoy their cities by walking, running or riding bicycles.

With the COVID-19 pandemic, such an initiative could even be considered for more than one day, particularly as we found out that it is possible for many of us to work from home. But perhaps, such a measure will only be needed until electric cars are the norm rather than the exception.

Antanas received Bogotá D.C. in chaos, where many people did not

---

[107] Corpovisionarios, Dónde hemos trabajado? www.corpovisionarios.org

respect local laws (including traffic signs, traffic lights and not littering), with high levels of poverty and unemployment, and the legacy of conflict reflected in high levels of stress, anxiety and the constant honking of cars.

Add to that seven million inhabitants, many of them from diverse ethnicities and regions of Colombia, looking for better life opportunities, with many also displaced by the conflict. If anyone else looked at that picture, it could seem a recipe for disaster.

Mockus believed that Colombians were more afraid of being ridiculed than getting a fine (I think this is true not just of Colombians but most people), so he hired hundreds of mimes to make fun of traffic violators. The mimes inspired the laughs and smiles of Bogotanos daily.

Pedagogic exercises like the above meant that in a short period, most people in Bogotá were respecting the road and traffic signs, the public spaces were cleaner, the air and noise pollution decreased, and constant car honking was no longer the norm.

Mockus made many of us dream that we could live in a society where sustainability, pluralism, fairness, respect for the other and enjoyment are always part of the equation.

"One of the most important lessons of Antanas Mockus's views on achieving peace in Colombia is that it makes no sense to sign formal agreements at the top if citizens themselves do not interiorise a new civic consciousness."[108]

Most Colombians also came to know Jaime Garzón (RIP, 1960– 1999). Jaime belongs in the category of the immortal ones. He was, among others, a comedian, journalist, and peace activist.

Colombians' appreciation and love for Jaime Garzón grew throughout the 90s with the political satire he used through different television programs and characters he created, including his depictions of the Colombian workers most often discriminated against and not heard.

The satire and criticism were not only of the government and those in power, but everyone. He ridiculed the guerrilla, the paramilitary, the drug cartels, the military, the political parties, the U.S. ambassadors in Colombia, the hippies, the snobs. No one was safe from his satire.

---

[108] F Forman 'Rethinking Cultural Agency: The Significance of Antanas Mockus' Cambridge, MA: (Harvard University Press, 2016) Chapter 5. Social Norms and the Cross-Border Citizen: From Adam Smith to Antanas Mockus p. 19

Jaime Garzón showed us the importance of hearing one another. To be better informed, to question our perspectives, to open peace dialogues as many times until we are able to see ourselves in the mirror, and to see the need for reconciliation so that we could aim to reach peaceful, inclusive solutions.

Jaime believed in democracy and that a peaceful, fairer and just society was possible.

Colombia's extreme right-wing killed him in 1999. It is still very difficult to comprehend why someone who brought so many laughs, entertainment and happiness to Colombian households, and someone who was not part of our binary lenses, was killed.

Jaime's death was one of the reasons I left my native Colombian land.

As has happened to many others worldwide, they killed the man, but not his ideas.

To fight, yes, but only with our ideas and reasoning, and not with guns.

To choose tolerance over prejudice.

To learn to share rather than to accumulate.

To choose love over hate.

One of my fondest memories at Universidad Externado de Colombia, apart from being with classmates from la Guajira to the Amazonas, was the privilege to have had Fernando Hinestrosa Daza (RIP) as professor of the subject Obligations (civil law) in my third year of law studies.

Hinestrosa Daza was an academic, a humanist, magistrate of Colombia's High Supreme Court, and university chancellor. He was wise. He believed in democratic values and in pluralistic and conciliatory approaches.

The respect for the dignity of human beings was something that he in subtle ways showed. Respectfully and caringly, in an almost fatherly way, he would always take the time after lectures to answer more questions while walking through the corridors of the university, despite how busy he must have been.

Hinestrosa Daza remembered the names of every one of his students, and he always called you by your name without reading it from a list. He had a playful, almost childish kind of face that contrasted with his inquisitive look, and deep, paused voice: "If you break it, you pay for it."

Our global financial and economic system with its stock exchanges, corporations and billionaires is operating not only as an obsolete system, but a broken one.

And as we keep finding excuses to not pay for the damage caused, more ecological and social devastation will occur. Or, we change.

I have never forgotten my roots. My parents, younger brother and many of my extended family and friends live in Colombia, and if it wasn't because of the coronavirus pandemic, my little family and I should have been in Colombia visiting them in 2020.

The enforced lockdown and my wife's patience allowed me to write this book though.

I'm married to a fourth-generation Aussie born in Melbourne, Australia. She is a writer, editor and speaker of four languages, with ancestors from the United Kingdom. She has been my best mate since we met in 2005. Together we have visited Colombia several times. She loves my forgotten land too.

I think the perception and the association that Colombia is Pablo Escobar and cocaine is changing. Indeed, the richness of Colombia is in its biodiversity. It hosts close to 10% of the planet's biodiversity, in 314 types of ecosystems, and ranks first in bird and orchid species diversity and second in its diversity of plants, butterflies, freshwater fish and amphibians.[109]

The biodiversity of Colombia is not just in its flora and fauna. Colombia has 87 different ethnic groups and 65 different languages. The Amazon region is home of over 70 Indigenous ethnic groups.

For instance, in the north of Colombia, in the Department of La Guajira, are the Wayuu, and in the Department of Magdalena, the Tayrona descendants include the Arhuaco, Wiwa, Kogi and Kankuamo, in La Sierra Nevada de Santa Marta and its "Lost City", the Ciudad Perdida.[110]

The richness and beauty of Colombian Indigenous cultures is seen at the gold museums, including the unique Gold Museum of Bogota[111], and the legacy of Gerardo Reichel-Dolmatoff, an anthropologist and archaeologist who lived from 1912 to 1994, as well as that of his wife

---

[109] United Nations, Convention on Biological Diversity
https://www.cbd.int/countries/profile/?country=co
[110] Procolombia, Colombia's Indigenous groups: https://www.colombia.co/en/colombia-country/colombia-facts/colombias-indigenous-groups/
[111] Red Cultural del Banco de la República en Colombia, Museo del oro y red de museos regionals: https://www.banrepcultural.org/cultura-del-cuidado/museo-del-oro-y-museos-regionales

the ethnologist Alicia Dussán Maldonado.

Reichel-Dolmatoff believed in research in holistic terms. He expressed that if humanity wanted to survive and stop the destruction of nature, it would be worth looking to the past and emulating some of the models developed by Indigenous societies.

Gerardo had also vast knowledge of botany and linguistics, a command of Spanish, English, German and French, and an understanding of several Indigenous languages.

He and Alicia studied Indigenous communities for over 50 years, and they authored over 200 titles on Colombian archaeology and anthropology. Gerardo worked for Colombian universities, was a professor of anthropology for the University of California and was a visiting professor at Cambridge University.[112]

The diversity of Colombia is also in its variety of traditional dances, including El San Juanero, El Joropo, La Cumbia, El Porro, El Currulao and La Guabina.

A cultural element that identifies us is definitely dancing. Every celebration involves it.

The Colombian love of dancing is also reflected in the different types of music, including Vallenato, Salsa, Merengue, Champeta, as well as Colombian rock, pop, urban and hip hop music. Disney even made a movie based on much of this – the widely popular Encanto.

Colombia's contribution to the world is also, therefore, in the arts and science. Singers like Shakira or Juanes are recognised worldwide not only for their music, but their social consciousness.

Shakira with her foundation "Pies Descalzos" (the Barefoot Foundation) supports Colombian education, and Juanes has been outspoken on the inequalities and violence in Colombia. His foundation "Mi sangre" (My blood) was established to help victims of anti-personnel mines.

And of course, there is Gabo – Gabriel García Marquéz (1927–2014), who received the Nobel prize in literature in 1982. Colombians and so many others worldwide love the magical realism of his books, including Cien Años de Soledad (One Hundred Years of Solitude) and El Amor en los Tiempos del Cólera (Love in the Time of Cholera).

Fernando Botero, the figurative painter and sculptor that brought

---

[112] A Oyuela–Caicedo 'Gerardo Reichel Dolmatoff' https://www.cambridge.org/core/services/aop-cambridge-core/content/view/575A20448B245C0852743AE11F041BA0/S0002731600049994a.pdf/gerardo_reicheldolmatoff_19121994.pdf

back the love and appreciation of curves – some may say, to paraphrase a Spanish expression, the love for "the chubby ones."

Botero is one of the most recognised contemporary artists from Latin America, and his art can be seen not only in the Botero museums in Bogota and his hometown of Medellin, Colombia, but also in different cities around the world, including Park Avenue in New York City and the Champs-Élysées in Paris.

In science, there is Rodolfo Llinas, a neuroscientist who has published hundreds of scientific articles and has worked in many different universities in the U.S. He was also the Chairman of NASA's Neurolab Science Working Group. More recently, Diana Trujillo an aerospace engineer who leads the engineering team at the NASA Jet Propulsion Laboratory, oversaw the robotic arm of the Perseverance rover.

Fellow Colombians living abroad may get upset because people usually mention cocaine. I've been there too. It is a stigma that we Colombians carry. A stigma that is very visible going through customs on international flights.

Having lived already over two decades in Australia, I have realised most people mention cocaine or Pablo Escobar out of good faith, to start or keep a conversation, not from a negative or judging point of view, and perhaps in many cases because this is the only thing they've ever heard about Colombia given what has historically been portrayed in the mainstream media and yes, Hollywood films. It's hard, but hopefully, with more and more Colombians across the world doing amazing things, and more and more people around the world counting Colombians as friends, this will change.

When I left Colombia in 2001 and went to Australia, I wanted to learn English and travel the world. I fell in love with Australia, and with Melbourne as a beautifully multicultural city and the home of the Australian Open, as well as the friendliness and openness of Melburnians.

When my parents came to Australia to visit before the Global Financial Crisis of 2007/2008, what struck them most was seeing people's smiles, and that Aussies seemed genuinely happy.

Since the GFC though, I have started to see how Australia is changing. When before it was hard to find any person experiencing homelessness on the streets of the Australian capital cities, there are now more and more. People's smiles seem to unfortunately no longer be the norm. I hope I'm wrong.

Social and economic inequalities are not only a problem of low-income countries or regions such as those in South and Central America, Africa or Southeast Asia, but also the high-income countries.

For instance, the poverty levels of and discrimination towards Australian Aboriginals are undeniable. However, many Australians acknowledge the past and want to see a true, open and honest reconciliation process between Aboriginal and non-Aboriginal people.

I think most Australians know that we must be able to properly acknowledge the past and current wrongdoings and have started seeing that the value of reconciliation is not only for Aboriginal Nations but for all of us who call Australia home – we must compensate, and we need to heal.[113]

The negative treatment of Indigenous and Aboriginal Nations in Australia has unfortunately also extended to refugees and asylum seekers. This applies not only to Australia but historically many countries worldwide. It is perhaps fair to say that that it reflects who we currently are as a species.

My intention is not to point fingers or shame nations like Australia, nor our leaders and institutions. Given that Australia is a relatively new nation from the perspective of European settlers, the discrimination and unjust treatment towards Indigenous communities is perhaps more evident.

Indeed, Captain James Cook "discovered" Australia around 1770. If we compare him with Cristopher Columbus who "discovered the New World", the Americas, in 1492, the difference of a few hundred years is an important time difference that could be argued served to help the new settlers to destroy and stigmatise the Indigenous communities of Central and South America.

The realisation that most Indigenous communities throughout the world have received and unfortunately continue to receive similar and, in many cases, worse treatment, may help to build more consciousness and hopefully lead to more education to tackle our common discriminatory and racist views towards Indigenous communities and minority groups.

---

[113] Uluru Statement Org https://ulurustatement.org/;Reconciliation Australia 'Five Dimensions of Reconciliation' https://www.reconciliation.org.au/what-is-reconciliation/; Nillumbik Reconciliation Group 'Imagination Declaration' https://nrg.org.au/events/imagination-declaration/; The Ngaga-dji Koorie Youth Council Report https://www.ngaga-djiproject.org.au/the-report

I think, like many others, that we could write a different story. We could live in a different reality. After all, humanity has always risen to the challenge. Our current global challenges, including climate change, are an opportunity.

It is our duty as a civil society to take accountability for our acts and make sure governments, corporations, shareholders and billionaires are accountable for theirs too.

ABOUT THE AUTHOR

Julián Correcha Rodríguez was born in Colombia, South America in 1975. He holds a Bachelor Law from the Universidad Externado de Colombia, a Postgraduate Diploma as Specialist in Public Management and Administrative Institutions from the Universidad de los Andes, and a Master of Human Rights Law from the University of Melbourne. Julián lived in Colombia and worked as a commercial lawyer until 2001 when he decided to migrate to Australia.

He has worked "down under" in different roles including Foundation Legal Studies teacher, Assessment Officer, Paralegal, Administration Officer, and Information and Engagement Officer for the Human Rights Commission in the state of Victoria. He has also worked as social and market research telephone interviewer for social and market research companies, and is proud to have also had the opportunity to work as a replenishment officer for a department store, and a cleaner on and off for several years to support himself and his family.

Julián holds dual citizenship from both Colombia and Australia, and perhaps like many migrants who have lived for long periods in other countries, he identifies as a citizen of the world. He believes that given the global challenges we have created, including climate change, this is the mindset required to tackle them.

BIBLIOGRAPHY

Alston P and Goodman R (2013) *'International Human Rights'*, Oxford University Press 4th ed.

Alston P (2005) *The 'Not-A-Cat' Syndrome:* Can the International Human Rights Regime Accommodate Non-State Actors? *Non-State Actors and Human Rights.*

Arriagada NB, Palmer AJ and others *'Unprecedent smoke-related health burden associated with the 2019-20 bushfires in eastern Australia'* (The Medical Journal of Australia MJA Vol 213, Issue 6 (282-283) https://onlinelibrary.wiley.com/doi/10.5694/mja2.50545

Australian Broadcasting Corporation, *'Fight for Planet A: Our Climate Challenge'* Aug 16, 2020.

Australian Broadcasting Corporation, *'Rest Super Fund Commits to net-zero emission investments after Brisbane man sues'* 2 Nov 2020 https://www.abc.net.au/news/2020-11-02/rest-super-commits-to-net-zero-emmissions/12840204

Bendell J (2020) *'Deep Adaptation: A Map for Navigating Climate Tragedy'* (Institute of Leadership and Sustainability (IFLAS) University of Cumbria UK (2nd Edition released 27 July 2020   http://lifeworth.com/deepadaptation.pdf.

Boochani, Behrouz (2018) *'No Friend but The Mountains'*, Picador.

Boyd, DR (2–17) *The Rights of Nature: A legal revolution that could save the world* ECW Press.

Carbon Emissions to Protect Young People, Future Generations and Nature, PLoS ONE (2013) http://journals.plos.org/plosone/article?id=10.1371/journal.pone.0081648

Chinkin, C (2019) 'Adoption of 1325 resolution' in S.E Davies and J. True (Eds). Oxford Handbook of Women, Peace and Security, New York: Oxford University Press.

Chinkin, C and Kaldor, M (2013) *'Gender and New Wars'*, 67 (1) Journal of International Affairs.

Chinkin, C and Rees, M (2016) 'Exposing the Gendered Myth of Post Conflict Transition: The Transformative Power of Economic and Social Rights', 48 New York University Journal of International Law and Politics.

Climate Action Tracker Org: https://climateactiontracker.org/countries/brazil/

Constitución Política de Colombia 1991.

Constitute Project Org https://www.constituteproject.org/constitution/Colombia_2005.pdf

C40 Cities Climate Leadership Group https://www.c40.org/

Corpovisionarios, Dónde hemos trabajado? www.corpovisionarios.org

Deloitte 'Clarity in Financial Reporting – Disclosure of climate-related risks' (A&A Accounting technical Feb 2020) https://www2.deloitte.com/content/dam/Deloitte/au/Documents/audit/deloitte-au-audit-clarity-disclosure-climate-related-risks-070220.pdf

Dembour, Marie-Benedicte (2010) *What are human rights? Four Schools of Thought*, p32, Human Rights Quarterly 1.

Doctors for the Environment Australia, letter dated 11 August 2020 addressed to Hon. Scoot Morrison, MP, Prime Minister of Australia https://www.dea.org.au/wp-content/uploads/2020/08/2020-08-06-Healthy-Recovery-Letter-_-Scott-Morrison-PM.pdf

Enloe, C (2014) 'Understanding militarism, militarisation, and the linkages with globalisation'. Using a Feminist Curiosity, in Gender and Militarism Analysing the Links to Strategize for Peace.

Earth's Endangered Creatures http://www.earthsendangered.com/search-regions3.asp?mp=1&search=1&sgroup=allgroups&ID=92Grainne D, Keohanne R and Sabel C 'New *Modes of Pluralist Governance'* (NYU Journal of International Law and Politics 45).

Food and Agriculture Organization of the United Nations (FAO) 'Tackling Climate Change through Livestock, A Global Assessment of Emissions and Mitigation Opportunities' (FAO 2013).

Forbes https://www.forbes.com/real-time-billionaires/#267e8bdc3d78

Forman F (2016) 'Rethinking Cultural Agency: The Significance of Antanas Mockus' Cambridge, MA: Harvard University Press.

Freedom House, Government Accountability & Transparency *'A well-functioning democracy requires strong safeguards against official corruption'* https://freedomhouse.org/issues/government-accountability-transparency

Galloway S (2018) 'Why Amazon, Apple, Facebook and Google Need to be Disrupted' Feb 8 2018 https://www.esquire.com/newspolitics/a15895746/bust-big-tech-silicon-valley/

Gomis, E. Lonnoy, T. Maycock, M. Tignor, and T. Waterfield (eds.)]. In Press https://www.ipcc.ch/sr15/chapter/spm/

Goodall J (2020) *'Remarks for World Animal Day 2020'* 4 October 2020, available at https://www.youtube.com/watch?v=9le192CyzYY

Hansen J and Others (2013) "Assessing "Dangerous Climate Change": Required Reduction of Greenham T *'Money is a social relationship.'* TEDx Leiden, 29 November 2012, available at https://www.youtube.com/watch?v=f1pS1emZP6A

Hansen J and Others (2016) "Ice melt, sea level rise and superstorms: evidence from paleoclimate data, climate modeling, and modern observations that 2°C global warming could be dangerous". Atmos. Chem. Phys. https://www.atmos-chem-phys.net/16/3761/2016/;

Hansen J and Others (2017) *"Young people's burden: requirement of negative CO2 emissions"*. Earth Syst. Dynam. https://www.earth-syst-dynam.net/8/577/2017/

Harari YN (2015) '*Sapiens, A Brief History of Humankind*' Penguin Random House, UK.

Harari YN (2017) '*Homo Deus, A brief History of Tomorrow*' Penguin Random House, UK.

Harari YN (2018) '*21 lessons for the 21*st *Century*' Jonathan Cape, London.

Hathaway JC & Foster M '*The Law of Refugee Status Second Edition*' (Cambridge University Press 2014).

Hiller R 'Militarised parenthood in Israel (Women Peacemakers Program [wpm] 2014.

Huntley R 'How to talk about Climate Change in a Way That Makes a Difference' (Murdock Books 2020).

Independent Commission for the Reform of International Corporate Taxation '*The OECD has not delivered. The world needs and answer now, not further delays*' https://www.icrict.com/press-release/2020/10/11/52n5njz8ja42ukkws0z7vgppuuse4b

Independent Commission for the Reform of International Corporate Taxation '*International Corporate Tax reform: Towards a fair and comprehensive solution*' (October 2019) https://static1.squarespace.com/static/5a0c602bf43b5594845abb81/t/5d979e6dc5f7cb7b66842c49/1570217588721/ICRICT-INTERNATIONAL+CORPORATE+TAX+REFORM.pdf

Intergovernmental Panel on Climate change (IPCC), 2018: Summary for Policymakers. In: Global Warming of 1.5°C. An IPCC Special Report on the impacts of global warming of 1.5°C above pre-industrial levels and related global greenhouse gas emission pathways, in the context of strengthening the global response to the threat of climate change, sustainable development, and efforts to eradicate poverty / Projected Climate Change, Potential Impacts and Associated Risks (B.5.2) [Masson-Delmotte, V., P. Zhai, H.-O. Pörtner, D. Roberts, J. Skea, P.R. Shukla, A. Pirani, W. Moufouma-Okia, C. Péan, R. Pidcock, S. Connors, J.B.R. Matthews, Y. Chen, X. Zhou, M.I.

International Covenant on Civil and Political Rights (ICCPR) https://www.ohchr.org/en/professionalinterest/pages/ccpr.aspx.

International Covenant on Economic, Social and Cultural Rights, opened for signature 16 December 1966, 993 UNTS 3. https://www.ohchr.org/en/professionalinterest/pages/cescr.aspx

International Convention on the Elimination of All Forms of Discrimination Against Women, CEDAW opened for signature 1 March 1980 https://www.ohchr.org/EN/ProfessionalInterest/Pages/CEDAW.aspx

International Convention on the Elimination of All Forms of Racial Discrimination, opened for signature 21 December 1965, [1975] ATS 40 (entered into force 4 January 1969).

International Monetary Fund (IMF), About the IMF, https://www.imf.org/en/About

International Monetary Fund (IMF), The IMF and the Sustainable Development Goals https://www.imf.org/en/Capacity-Development/what-we-do

Kirsch S (2018) *'Engaged Anthropology, Politics Beyond the Text'*, University of California Press.

Knox JH (2014) 'Climate Ethics and Human Rights' 5 (special issue), Journal of Human Rights and Environment.

Knox JH (2018) 'The Paris Agreement as a Human Rights Treaty' in Akande et al. (eds), *Human Rights and the 21ˢᵗ Century Challenges: Poverty, Conflict and the Environment*, Oxford University Press.

Kyoto Protocol to the United Nations Framework Convention on Climate Change (1998)

Langton M (2018) 'Welcome to Country: A travel guide to Indigenous Australia', Hardie Grant Travel.

Nillumbik Reconciliation Group *'Imagination Declaration'* https://nrg.org.au/events/imagination-declaration/

Nyuol Vincent D with Nader C *'The boy who wouldn't Die'* (Fairfax 2013).

Office of the United Nations High Commissioner for Refugees – Figures forcibly displaced people as of 2020 https://www.unhcr.org/figures-at-a-glance.html

Office of the United Nations High Commissioner for Refugees – Figures forcibly displaced people as of 2015 https://www.unhcr.org/576408cd7

Optional Protocol to the Convention on the Elimination of All Forms of Discrimination Against Women (2000)

Oxford Dictionary Online https://en.oxforddictionaries.com/definition/universality

Oyuela–Caicedo, A *'Gerardo Reichel Dolmatoff'* https://www.cambridge.org/core/services/aop-cambridge-core/content/view/575A20448B2 45C0852743 AE 11 F0 41BA0/S0002731600049994a.pdf/gerardo_reicheldolmatoff_19121994.pdf

Pascoe, B *'Dark Emu'* (2014) Magabala Books Aboriginal Corporation, Broome, Western Australia.

Pickett K and Wilkinson R (2009) *'The Spirit Level'* Penguin, London.

Pickett K and Wilkinson R (2014) *'The Spirit Level Authors: Why Society is More Unequal Than Ever,'* The Guardian 9 March 2014: https://www.theguardian.com/commentisfree/2014/mar/09/society-unequal-the-spirit-level

Preventing conflict transforming justice securing the peace – Global Study on the Implementation of United Nations Security Council resolution 1325 (2015).

Procolombia, Colombia's Indigenous groups: https://www.colombia.co/en/colombia-country/colombia-facts/colombias-indigenous-groups/

Rajamani L (2018) Human Rights in the Climate Change Regime: From Rio to Paris. In John H. Knox and Ramin Pejan (eds), The Human Right to a Healthy Environment, Cambridge University Press.

Raworth K (2017) 'Seven ways to Think Like a 21st Century Economist', Chelsea Green Publishing.

Reconciliation Australia *'Five Dimensions of Reconciliation'* https://www.reconciliation.org.au/what-is-reconciliation/

Red Cultural del Banco de la República en Colombia, Museo del Oro y Red de Museos Regionales: https://www.banrepcultural.org/cultura-del-cuidado/museo-del-oro-y-museos-regionales

Refugee Council of Australia: *'Seven years on: An Overview of Australia's Offshore Processing Policies'* (July 2020) https://www.refugeecouncil.org.au/wp-content/uploads/2020/07/RCOA-Seven-Years-On.pdf

Rodman S (2015) 'How to talk to your kids about your divorce', Adams Media.

Royal Commission into National Natural Disaster Arrangements Report 28 Oct 2020, p5 https://naturaldisaster.royalcommission.gov.au/publications/royal-commission-national-natural-disaster-arrangements-report

Rodríguez-Garavito, Cesar *'Business and Human Rights: Beyond the End of the Beginning'* 2017 Cambridge University Press.

Ruggie JG (2013) 'Just Business Multinational Corporations and Human Rights', W.W Norton & Company Ltd.

Ruggie JG (2017) 'The Multinational as a Global Institution: Power, Authority and Relative Autonomy' (Regulation and Governance).

Sabin Center for Climate Change Law – Climate Change Litigation Databases http://climatecasechart.com/

Sagan, C (1997) *'Billions and Billions – Thoughts on Life and Death at the Brink of the Millennium'*, Random House New York.

Shepherd L (2016) 'Making war safe for women? National Action Plans and the militarisation of the Women, Peace and Security agenda,' 37 (3) International Political Science Review.

Shosana Z (2019) *'The Age of Surveillance Capitalism'*, New York: Public Affairs.

Smith, A 1892, *'The Theory of Moral Sentiments'* (London: George Bell & Sons. York St, Covent Garden, and New York 1892). Digitised by Google.

Statista – Worldwide Automobile Production https://www.statista.com/statistics/262747/worldwide-automobile-production-since-2000/

Stockholm International Peace Research Institute (SIPRI) https://www.sipri.org/media/press-release/2020/global-military-expenditure-sees-largest-annual-increase-decade-says-sipri-reaching-1917-billion

Svedberg B, Chinkin C, Mlinarevic G, True J, Rees M and Isakovic NP (2017) 'A Feminist Perspective on Post-conflict Restructuring and Recovery – the Study of Bosnia and Herzegovina, Women's International League for Peace and Freedom.

The Economist Intelligence Unit (2015) The Road from Principles to Practice: Today's challenges for Business in Respecting Human Rights.

The National Aeronautics and Space Administration- NASA *'Facts - Vital Signs'* https://climate.nasa.gov/vital-signs/carbon-dioxide/

The National Aeronautics and Space Administration- NASA *'The causes of climate change'* https://climate.nasa.gov/causes/

The Ngaga-dji Koorie Youth Council Report https://www.ngaga-djiproject.org.au/the-report

The Sydney Morning Herald, full transcript Donald Trump and Malcolm Turnbull full conversation (August 4 2017), http://www.smh.com.au/world/full-transcript-donald-trump-and-malcolm-turnbull-telephone-conversation-20170803-gxp13g.html

Uluru Statement Org https://ulurustatement.org/;.

United Nations *CEDAW History* http://www.un.org/womenwatch/daw/cedaw/history.htm

United Nations *Charter of the United Nations* (October 1945) https://www.un.org/en/sections/un-charter/chapter-i/index.html

United Nations Committee on the Elimination of Discrimination against Women *'General recommendation No.30 on Women in conflict prevention, conflict and post-conflict situations'* https://www.ohchr.org/documents/hrbodies/cedaw/gcomments/cedaw.c.cg.30.pdf

United Nations, Convention on Biological Diversity https://www.cbd.int/countries/profile/?country=co

United Nations, Convention on the Rights of Persons with Disabilities, opened for signature 30 March 2007, [2008] ATS 12 (entered into force 3 May 2008) https://www.un.org/development/desa/disabilities/convention-on-the-rights-of-persons-with-disabilities.html

United Nations, Convention Relating to the Status of Refugees, opened for signature 28 July 1951, [1954] ATS 5 (entered into force 22 April 1954) https://www.unhcr.org/en-au/1951-refugee-convention.html

United Nations, Declaration on the Rights of Indigenous People (2007) https://www.un.org/development/desa/indigenouspeoples/declaration-on-the-rights-of-indigenous-peoples.html

United Nations, Facts and Figures Hunger: https://www.un.org/sustainabledevelopment/hunger/

United Nations Framework Convention on Climate Change (1992)

United Nations *Growth in United Nations membership*, 1945 – present http://www.un.org/en/sections/member-states/growth-united-nations-membership-1945-present/index.html

United Nations *'Guiding Principles on Business and Human Rights'* The Corporate Responsibility to Respect Human Rights 12 https://www.ohchr.org/Documents/Publications/GuidingPrinciplesBusinessHR_EN.pdf

United Nations *International Convention on the Elimination of All Forms of Discrimination Against Women*, opened for signature 1 March 1980
https://www.ohchr.org/EN/ProfessionalInterest/Pages/CEDAW.aspx

United Nations *International Covenant on Civil and Political Rights*, opened for signature 16 December 1966, [1980] ATS 23 https://www.ohchr.org/en/instruments-mechanisms/instruments/international-covenant-civil-and-political-rights

United Nations *International Covenant on Economic, Social and Cultural Rights*, opened for signature 16 December 1966, 993 UNTS 3,
https://www.ohchr.org/en/professionalinterest/pages/cescr.aspx;

United Nations Office of the High Commissioner for Human Rights – Status of Ratification of 18 International Human Rights Treaties Interactive Dashboard
http://indicators.ohchr.org/

United Nations Office of the High Commissioner, *The Core International Human Rights Instruments and their monitoring bodies* http://www.ohchr.org/EN/ProfessionalInterest/Pages/CoreInstruments.aspx

United Nations Office of the High Commissioner, *What are human rights? Universal and inalienable* www.ohchr.org/EN/Issues/Pages/WhatareHuman Rights.aspx

United Nations Paris Agreement (2015) https://unfccc.int/sites/default/files/english_paris_agreement.pdf

United Nations Refugee Agency UNHCR – *Figures at a Glance*
https://www.unhcr.org/figures-at-a-glance.html

United Nations Refugee Agency UNHCR *Global Trends Forced Displacement in 2015*
https://www.unhcr.org/576408cd7

United Nations Refugee Agency UNHCR *Handbook on Procedures and Criteria for Determining Refugee Status under the 1951 Convention and the 1967 Protocol relating to the Status of Refugees*, UN Doc. HCR/IP/4/Eng/REV.3 (2011) ("Handbook")

United Nations Security Council Resolution 1325 (2000) https://www.unwomen.org/en/docs/2000/10/un-security-council-resolution-1325

United Nations, Sustainable Development Goals https://www.un.org/sustainabledevelopment/

United Nations *The Foundation of International Human Rights Law*
http://www.un.org/en/sections/universal-declaration/foundation-international-human-rights-law/index.html

United Nations Women *Preventing Conflict Transforming Justice Securing the Peace* A global study on the implementation of United Nations Security Council Resolution 1325 (2015)

Weissbrodt D and Krugger M 'Human Rights Responsibilities of Business as Non-State Actors', in Alston P, *Non-State Actors and Human Rights*.

Whitman w '*Song of Myself' (1892 version)*
https://www.poetryfoundation.org/poems/45477/song-of-myself-1892-version

Wilkinson K *'How empowering women and girls can help stop global warming.'* TED Palm Spring California, November 2018, available at https://www.youtube.com/watch?v=vXlJEcrinwg

World Bank, Measuring Poverty https://www.worldbank.org/en/topic/poverty

World Health Organization, Cholera – Key facts https://www.who.int/news-room/fact-sheets/detail/cholera

World Health Organization Health and Development https://www.who.int/hdp/poverty/en/

World Health Organization, Influenza (seasonal) https://www.who.int/news-room/fact-sheets/detail/influenza-(seasonal)

World Health Organisation, Malaria – Key facts https://www.who.int/news-room/fact-sheets/detail/malaria